The Case of Mrs. Surratt

The Case of Mrs. Surratt

Her Controversial Trial and Execution for Conspiracy in the Lincoln Assassination

by Guy W. Moore

Norman : University of Oklahoma Press

Library of Congress Catalog Card Number: 54-5928

 Composed and printed at Norman, Oklahoma, U.S.A., by the University of Oklahoma Press. First edition.

To my Wife, who made it possible

Acknowledgments

THE AUTHOR desires to express his sincere appreciation to the staff of the National Archives in Washington, D. C., especially to Dr. Richard Wood, chief, Army Section, War Department Records, and Mr. Raymond Flynn, archivist in the War Records section, for assistance in obtaining and examining archival material relative to this case.

Also to the staffs of the Library of Congress and the Washington Public Library, especially to the Manuscript Division and the Newspaper Room of the Library of Congress and to the Washingtoniana Division of the Public Library.

Also to Monsignor E. P. McAdams, recognized Washington authority on this case, who gave freely of his time and opened to the writer his personal collection of materials assembled over the past forty years.

Also to Colonel Julian E. Raymond, until recently post commander, Fort Lesley J. McNair, whose manuscript history of the Fort and whose research into incidents surrounding the hanging of Mrs. Surratt brought to the writer some facts not generally known.

At the University of Oklahoma the author is especially indebted to Dr. Edwin C. McReynolds, associate professor, Department of History, for giving generously of his time in the direction of research upon which this book is based. Thanks are also due to Dr. A. B. Sears, chairman of the Department of History at the University, and to Dr. A. K. Christian of the same department.

GUY W. MOORE

Washington, D. C.
January 21, 1954

Contents

Illustrations

The Case of Mrs. Surratt

CHAPTER I

Mrs. Surratt and the Assassination of President Lincoln

WHEN the woman was hanged almost nobody doubted her guilt. It was an accepted fact that Mrs. Surratt was one of those who helped John Wilkes Booth when he assassinated President Lincoln. The government had proclaimed it; the newspapers asserted her part in the conspiracy. After a trial which dragged on for six weeks, and after lengthy testimony on both sides, she had been found guilty. Outside her circle of family and friends, probably less than a dozen people entertained any real doubts about the verdict. But these doubts began to be heard as soon as (indeed, before) the execution was finished, and, with the passing of time, the verdict of guilt has come increasingly under fire. As more and more facts have come to light, her guilt has become more and more uncertain, and books have been written to prove her innocence.

What is the truth about Mrs. Surratt? Was she guilty or innocent? It is the purpose of this book to answer this question, insofar as the facts permit an answer. In the light of the evidence offered at her trial and from evidence which has emerged since, an effort will be made to explore the facts and to record them. In attempting to answer the question of her guilt and to establish the truth, it will be helpful to restate the main facts in Mrs. Surratt's life, to look in upon the people at the boardinghouse she kept in Washington, and to review the involved and protracted controversies which have raged about her name since her death that scorching Friday afternoon in July, 1865.

Mary Eugenia Jenkins Surratt was born about 1817, near Waterloo, on Calvert's manor, in Prince George's County, Maryland. Her father died when she was quite young. As she grew up she wanted more than a local education and, at her own insistence, was sent to a Catholic female seminary in Alexandria. Returning to her mother's home, she became an acknowledged belle in the locality and married John H. Surratt about 1835. The couple settled at Condon's Mill, near Glensboro, Maryland, on property Surratt had inherited from an uncle named Neale. For a time Surratt was a contractor on the Orange and Alexandria Railroad; later he returned to Maryland and his native county and bought a farm on which he established a tavern. A post office was opened at "Surratt's" and John H. Surratt was appointed postmaster, the place henceforth being called Surrattsville. Surratt being uneducated, most of the duties of the office devolved on his wife.

There were three children—a daughter and two sons. The eldest son, Isaac, went South at the outbreak of the Civil War. The daughter, Anna E., lived at home, and the other son, John H., Jr., was at St. Charles' College near Ellicott's Mills until his father's death in 1862, when he came home to serve out his father's term as postmaster.

Mary E. Surratt

Courtesy National Park Service

John H. Surratt, Sr., was known as a proslavery man, but was not looked upon as an open secessionist. He was inoffensive, good-tempered, and generally esteemed.[1]

When the elder Surratt died, the family fortunes were on the downgrade. Fifteen years after he had helped defend Mrs. Surratt against the charge of complicity in Lincoln's death, one of her attorneys gave us a brief, clear picture of the conditions facing the widow. At the opening of the war the family had had a "large plantation well-stocked and cultivated by numerous slaves" and a property in Washington, but the family suffered from the depredations of the army and its followers. The slaves disappeared; crops melted away. The plantation lay within the cordon of lines of protection thrown around Washington and became, in time, a barren waste. So, unable to support her family any longer in the country, Mrs. Surratt moved to Washington.[2]

Mrs. Surratt and her daughter Anna came to Washington on October 1, 1864. She had rented her tavern and what was left of the plantation to John M. Lloyd for five hundred dollars a year.[3] Her youngest son she left in charge at Surrattsville until the new tenant took over on the first day of December.[4]

As soon as she was established in her new home, Mrs.

[1] Washington *Evening Star,* May 12 and July 7, 1865. "Mary E. Surratt," article, *National Cyclopedia of American Biography, IV,* 347.

[2] John W. Clampitt, "The Trial of Mrs. Surratt," *North American Review,* Vol. CXXXI (September, 1880), 225.

[3] Washington *Evening Star,* July 7, 1865.

[4] David M. DeWitt, *The Assassination of Abraham Lincoln and Its Expiation,* 20.

Surratt began renting rooms. As she herself said later, "I came from Maryland and I had no way of living except by renting the rooms and taking in a few boarders. I advertised in the *Star* several times that I had rooms for rent."[5] And, again, "I wanted to get a few boarders as we had two back rooms, and I thought if I could get them filled, I could live."[6] The location of the house and the fact that she was not without friends augured well for the project. The house stood at 541 H Street—a central location, not far from the great National Hotel at Sixth and Pennsylvania, Ford's Theater on Eleventh Street, the Kirkwood House at Twelfth and the Avenue, and the Herndon House at Ninth and F streets. Furthermore, it was convenient to shopping and government areas downtown. Also important to Mrs. Surratt was the fact that Father Wiget, an old friend of the family, was at near-by Gonzaga College, and within easy walking distance was the Catholic Orphan Asylum where Miss Anna Ward, another old friend, was teaching.

Mrs. Surratt soon had two paying roomers: Miss Dean, a little girl eleven years old; and Miss Honora Fitzpatrick, the nineteen-year-old daughter of a collector for some of the Washington banks.[7] The next roomer to arrive was an old schoolmate of Mrs. Surratt's son John, Louis J. Weich-

[5] Mary E. Surratt, statement of April 28, 1865. Archives, Record Group 153, Records of the Judge Advocate General (War). Records Relating to Lincoln Assassination Suspects, Box No. 3, "S"-RB (JAO), P. 78–1865 (hereinafter cited as "Archives, RG 153, JAO," with box and item number only following).

[6] Mary E. Surratt, statement of April 17, 1865. Archives, RG 153, JAO, Box No. 3, "S"-RB, P. 79, No. 13.

[7] Statement of Colonel William P. Wood, Archives, RG 153, JAO, Box No. 1, unnumbered item.

mann, who, after a bit of teaching in Catholic institutions, was now working in the War Department. Still Mrs. Surratt needed more money, and she advertised in the *Star* three times for roomers, on November 30, December 8, and December 27. She also began serving meals on December 1. The Holahans moved in the first week in February, 1865. John Holahan had been born in Ireland, but had been in Washington fourteen years, and during the war was a bounty broker. With Holahan came his wife, Eliza, and their fourteen-year-old daughter.[8] Others came from time to time, but this completed the regular family circle at the boardinghouse.

It must have been a very crowded little boardinghouse. A narrow three-story and attic structure (which still stands and is but little changed), it had a high, outside flight of stairs leading up to the front door, and sat back from the street behind a row of large trees. On the street floor a hall led to the dining room and beyond it to the kitchen. On the second floor Mrs. Surratt's room was actually the back parlor, separated from the parlor in front of it only by folding doors. There were only two rooms on this floor.[9] On the third floor, there were three rooms. The Holahans had the front bedroom, directly over the front parlor, their daughter sleeping in a small room close by. Weichmann slept in a room back of the Holahans'.[10] In the attic there was additional space, and there Miss Anna Surratt and her cousin, Olivia Jenkins, slept when the latter was in town.

[8] *Trial of John H. Surratt in the Criminal Court for the District of Columbia*, I, 650, 688 (hereinafter cited as *Surratt Trial*).

[9] *Surratt Trial*, I, 376.

[10] *Ibid.*, 670.

Miss Fitzpatrick slept with Mrs. Surratt. When John H. Surratt was in town, he slept with Weichmann.[11]

It was into this household that John Wilkes Booth was introduced on January 1, 1865. The story of this young actor and his plots against Lincoln have been told many times by able writers, and only his relations with the Surratts concern us here. But it is vital to understand that Booth had in mind a scheme to abduct the President, and it was his desire to enlist the aid of young John Surratt that led him to make the latter's acquaintance. In substance, the background of Booth's activities, up to his entry into the Surratt home, is as follows:[12]

John Wilkes Booth was twenty-six years old, a successful actor, and remarkably handsome. He was "a stay-at-home champion" of the South,[13] and a fanatic on the question of race. When, in April, 1864, Grant stopped the exchange of prisoners in an effort to end the war more quickly, it occurred to Booth that if he could capture President Lincoln, he could ransom many of the Confederate prisoners in the North. He got his first recruits to his kidnap scheme in August, 1864, when Samuel Arnold and Michael O'Laughlin joined him. These two young men were schoolmates of Booth's, and both had fought in the Confederate ranks. Arnold was unemployed at this time, except when helping a brother on his farm near Hookstown, Maryland.

[11] Benn Pitman, *The Assassination of President Lincoln and the Trial of the Conspirators*, 116, testimony of Weichmann (hereinafter cited as Pitman, *The Trial)*.

[12] The account by DeWitt, *Assassination of Lincoln*, 1–37, is excellent.

[13] DeWitt, *Assassination of Lincoln*, 9.

O'Laughlin, who had taken the oath of allegiance in June, 1863, was in the produce business with his brother, William, working in Baltimore and Washington. After he had spellbound his two boyhood companions with the prospects of successfully carrying out his somewhat madcap abduction scheme, Booth went to Canada. But there is no proof that he told any of the Confederates there of his plan. Both Jacob Thompson and C. C. Clay, prominent Southern men who were on diplomatic missions, later disclaimed any knowledge of Booth or of his plot.

In the course of getting the lay of the land in southern Maryland over which he hoped to take his captive, Booth must have heard of young John H. Surratt. Surratt was at this time acting as dispatch carrier between Washington and Richmond, later asserting it was "a fascinating life" and making unkind remarks about the stupidity of the Union detectives who searched him from time to time.[14]

Anxious to meet Surratt, whose aid and knowledge of the country would be invaluable to him in his design on the President, Booth seized upon a chance meeting with Dr. Samuel Mudd to press for an introduction. Booth had met the Maryland country physician in November, 1864, while a guest of Mudd's neighbor, Dr. Queen. At that time he had asked Mudd about buying a riding horse, had spent the night at Mudd's home, and, the next day, had purchased a horse from George Gardiner, the doctor's neighbor.[15] On the evening of the twenty-third of Decem-

[14] John H. Surratt's Rockville, Md., lecture, printed in the Washington *Star,* December 8, 1870; reprinted in Clara E. Laughlin, *Death of Lincoln,* 222–49.

[15] Pitman, *The Trial,* 71.

ber, Booth, accidentally meeting Dr. Mudd on the Avenue, asked to be introduced to John Surratt, with whom he understood the doctor was acquainted. On their way to the Surratt house they met Surratt and Weichmann on the street. The party repaired to Booth's room in the National Hotel, had a few drinks, and talked of Booth's purchasing Mudd's farm, but probably did not discuss any plot against Lincoln. "This, it is agreed on all sides," says DeWitt, "was the first meeting of the two men who became the leading spirits of the plot to capture."[16] Booth did not see Surratt again until he called at the boardinghouse on New Year's Day, 1865.

It is interesting to note, in passing, that if this street meeting of Booth and Surratt was their first, there is evidence that it was not the first meeting of Booth and Weichmann, as is generally assumed. The Right Reverend Monsignor Edward P. McAdams,[17] in his recent history of St. Charles' College in Pikesville, Maryland, discloses that Weichmann, Booth, and Arnold attended college together for a time before Weichmann went to the more famous St. Charles' College west of Ellicott's, where he met John H. Surratt. Says Monsignor McAdams, "Historians writing of the assassination of President Lincoln have in nearly all instances failed to distinguish between the St. Charles' College at Pikesville, conducted by Father Waldron, and

[16] DeWitt, *Assassination of Lincoln*, 22.

[17] Monsignor McAdams is the outstanding local (Washington) authority on the case of Mrs. Surratt. He has more personal knowledge of the participants in the case than anyone now living. He knew Anna Surratt's husband and son, Miss Anna Ward, Father Wiget (who attended Mrs. Surratt on the scaffold), and others.

that conducted by the Sulpician Fathers on U. S. 40 opposite Doughoregan Manor, the country home of Charles Carroll of Carrollton."[18]

In all events, Surratt embraced Booth's scheme for abducting the President and added two more to the band: George Atzerodt, a former carriage painter from Port Tobacco, Maryland; and David Herold, a trifling, reckless boy of about nineteen, who had once worked as a drug clerk, but who found hunting along the Potomac far more to his liking. His knowledge of the country undoubtedly recommended him to Surratt. Booth himself added a man called Payne.[19] Lewis Payne was a huge youth of twenty, a Confederate veteran of Gettysburg (where he had been wounded), and a disillusioned deserter from a regiment of Virginia cavalry. He had been unable to find work in Baltimore, had no funds, and was far from his Florida home, when Booth saw him one day near the end of February. Booth's money and plans probably dazzled Payne; his loyalty to his benefactor never wavered afterward. And in Payne, Booth had the one man he could count on in any contingency.

One real but abortive attempt was made to capture Lincoln on or about March 20. After waiting for months, the

[18] Edward P. McAdams, *History of Saint Charles Borromeo Parish*, 1849–1949 (pamphlet), 31.

[19] "Payne" was the alias of Lewis Thornton Powell, but this was not known at first. Throughout the conspiracy trial the name Payne was used, and is still used in most discussions of Lincoln's death. When he signed the oath of allegiance in Baltimore on March 14, 1865, the spelling of the assumed name was "Paine." Original in the Archives, RG 153, JAO, Box No. 3, "W" RB, 31.

plotters laid in wait for the President, having heard he was to drive to the Soldiers Home. Lincoln was not in the carriage, however, and, afraid the government was aware of their plans, the band broke up. Arnold and O'Laughlin went to Baltimore, Arnold applying for a clerkship at Fortress Monroe, Virginia, and O'Laughlin going back to work for his brother. Booth went to New York, Surratt to Richmond. So much for the plot to capture Lincoln.

Very little time was left to John Wilkes Booth or anyone else to save the sinking Southern cause. On April 9, Lee surrendered at Appomattox. The thrilling news reached Washington at a late hour that night and was officially confirmed at daylight the next morning with the thunder of artillery and the joyous ringing of bells. The information set off a tremendous celebration. Government departments closed in honor of the day; the navy yard men paraded, and people thronged the streets, singing. The *Star* reported it "a day of jubilee," and said, "As we write the streets are filled with crowds of people almost wild with excitement over the great and glorious news of the surrender of Lee." It reported that two thousand persons were marching in a victory parade and that salutes, bell-ringings, and myriad bands were to be heard on all sides. It was the same story on the eleventh. On the twelfth, the *Star* reported a "grand illumination" and the speech of Lincoln the previous evening. On April 13 the *Star* announced an illumination called by the City Council for that night, which "bids fair to far exceed any previous demonstration of the sort ever witnessed here." And, on the fourteenth, the same paper described the "Grand Display" of the previous evening, with everything lit up, rockets dashing to meet the stars, and swarming, joyful people. In this same edition the *Star* also announced the benefit and last appearance of Laura Keene, at Ford's, in *The American Cousin.* And in the second edition it noted: "Lieut. Gen'l. Grant—President Lincoln and Lady, in company with Lieut. Gen'l. Grant, will occupy the State Box at Ford's Theater tonight."

But not everyone in Washington was so happy with the trend of events. On the evening of the eleventh, when Lincoln spoke to the crowd assembled outside the White House, he proposed that the vote be given to some of the most intelligent of the Negroes. To John Wilkes Booth this was the last straw; he suggested to his companion, Payne, who was also listening, that Payne shoot the President, and said, "That is the last speech he will ever make."[20] "This," DeWitt observes, "in all probability, was the moment when the design to kill first found lodgment in the brain of the baffled plotter."[21] On April 14, about noon, when he called at the Ford Theater for his mail, Booth learned that the President would be in the audience that night. After that, he acted swiftly.

He obtained horses for himself and Payne to use that night. He dropped by Mrs. Surratt's—arriving just as she was ready to depart—and gave her a package to take to Surrattsville for him. Then he went to Ford's Theater.[22]

Booth had access to the theater at all times—he had acted there, and was on good terms with everyone—and it

[20] Major Eckert's testimony, *Impeachment Investigation,* 40 Cong., 1 sess., *House Report No. 7,* 674 (hereinafter cited as *Imp. Inv*).

[21] DeWitt, *Assassination of Lincoln,* 40.

[22] *Surratt Trial,* I, 545–47, 612; DeWitt, *op. cit.,* 42.

is presumed that he entered the Presidential box that afternoon after the rehearsal. He bored a small hole in the door, cutting it clean with a penknife, and, using the penknife, cut a rough mortise in the wall plaster. A pine bar about three and one-half feet long was provided, apparently intended to brace the outer door (which had no lock) when one end was placed in the mortise, and thus protect the assassin from interference from the house. No one actually saw Booth making these preparations, but he was seen at the theater in the afternoon, and an iron-handled gimlet was found in his trunk at the National Hotel after the assassination.[23]

After Booth completed his preparations at Ford's, he went to Glover's Theater and wrote a letter explaining how he had long tried to capture the President but must now change his plans, and that he was sure posterity would justify him. This letter he signed "Men who love their country better than gold or life, J. W. Booth,—Payne,—Atzerodt,—Herold." Then he addressed it to the editor of the Washington *Intelligencer* and put it in his pocket. A little later he met his fellow-actor and boyhood chum, John Matthews. The two men walked together down Pennsylvania Avenue, Booth dramatically exclaiming (as Confederate prisoners passed by), "My God! My God! I no longer have a country. This is the end of constitutional liberty in America." Such was Booth's frame of mind on the night of the assassination. He requested Matthews to deliver the letter at a later hour that night.[24] Also, during the afternoon,

[23] Pitman, *The Trial,* 77, 78, 82, 111, 112.

[24] Testimony of John Matthews, *Imp. Inv.,* 782; also in interview in the Washington *Evening Star,* December 7, 1881.

Booth may have found time to drop by Kirkwood House where the Vice-President was staying, to leave a card reading:

> Don't wish to disturb you. Are you at home?
>
> J. Wilkes Booth[25]

At about eight o'clock that evening in the Herndon House, Booth and his fellow-conspirators held their last conference. Meeting in Payne's room with what was left of his little band,[26] Booth assigned to each the role he was to play: Payne was to kill Secretary of State Seward, Atzerodt to kill Vice-President Johnson. Herold was assigned to guide Payne out of the city after Seward was murdered. Booth reserved for himself the killing of the President and, shortly after nine o'clock, appeared at Ford's Theater.

Meanwhile, at the little house on H Street, all was quiet. Mrs. Surratt and Weichmann had returned from Surrattsville about half-past eight, Mrs. Surratt having

[25] Pitman, *The Trial,* 70. It has been assumed by most writers that Booth left this card. Internal evidence indicates he did. But this point was never really settled. Atzerodt once said Booth sent Herold and himself to Kirkwood House with this card, telling them they were to obtain a pass to go South. At the conspiracy trial, Robert Jones, the clerk who took the card, wasn't sure he had received it from Booth, saying, "I may have done so." See Colonel Foster's statement respecting Atzerodt, Archives, RG 153, JAO, Box 1, "F," 537. See also Pitman, *The Trial,* 70, 307.

[26] Arnold was clerking at Fortress Monroe; O'Laughlin was in Washington but was seen elsewhere. John Surratt later maintained that he was in Elmira, New York, on the assassination night, and his presence in Washington was never proved. Pitman, *The Trial,* 234, 240, 228.

been unable to transact her business there because the man she had gone to see had not shown up. John Holahan had asked his wife to go with him down to the Avenue to watch the big victory procession scheduled by arsenal employees for that night; his wife refused to go, so he went alone, getting back after Mrs. Surratt had returned.[27] They ate dinner and went to bed about ten o'clock, as usual.[28]

At approximately fifteen minutes past ten Booth shot the President.

At the same time Lewis Payne entered the Seward home on Lafayette Square, opposite the White House, and attacked the Secretary. He tried unsuccessfully to kill Seward, and, when the household became aroused, Payne fled. Atzerodt, whose reputation for cowardice was a laughing matter among those who knew him, went to the Kirkwood House where the Vice-President was staying, but did not go near his intended victim. After about five minutes at the Kirkwood, he rode away.

About two o'clock the following morning the boardinghouse doorbell rang violently several times in quick succession. Louis Weichmann, half-dressed, answered the door.[29] A number of uniformed men were demanding admittance, saying they wanted to search the house for John

[27] *Surratt Trial,* I, 674, testimony of John Holahan.

[28] Statement of Anna Surratt, Archives, RG 153, JAO, Box 3, "S" RB.

[29] *Surratt Trial,* I, 395. Pitman, *The Trial,* 116. Statement of officer McDevitt, in Ben ["Perley"] Poore, *Conspiracy Trial for the Murder of the President,* III, 382. Same in *Court Martial of the Lincoln Conspirators,* Restricted Material, Archives, Records of the Judge Advocate General, MM 2251 (hereinafter cited as "*Restricted Material*").

H. Surratt and John Wilkes Booth.[30] Weichmann walked back to Mrs. Surratt's room and told her of the officers' intention. She told him to let them come in.

When Mrs. Surratt came into the parlor, John Clarvoe, one of the searching party, asked, "When did you last see John Wilkes Booth?" She told him she had last seen Booth at two o'clock Friday afternoon; her son, two weeks before, but she had received a letter from him that day. Clarvoe said later, "She asked me what was the meaning of all this and said there were a great many mothers who did not know where their sons were. Said I, Mc., you tell her. . . ."[31] So while Clarvoe went upstairs to search for Booth and Surratt, Detective McDevitt told Mrs. Surratt that her son was believed to be the man who had attacked the Secretary of State as Booth shot the President. The detectives disturbed the occupants of the house, but found nothing suspicious and went away.

Just how the city detectives came to descend on Mrs. Surratt's so soon after the murder has caused much speculation. Eisenschiml speculates that maybe it was because a stableman named Fletcher recognized Atzerodt's saddle and bridle when they were brought into local police headquarters, and knew that Atzerodt had stayed at Mrs. Surratt's.[32] Probably the real answer is to be found in a newspaper interview with officer McDevitt, in the course of

[30] James A. McDevitt stated that he, Clarvoe, Lieutenant C. M. Skippon, with a squad of his men, and Mr. Donaldson of McDevitt's force were all at the Surratt house that night. All were metropolitan police, not government agents. *Surratt Trial,* I, 714.

[31] *Surratt Trial,* I, 698.

[32] Otto Eisenschiml, *Why Was Lincoln Murdered?*, 272–73.

which he said an actor (identity uncertain, but probably Booth's friend Matthews, who knew a lot about the actor's doings) told him "to keep an eye" on Mrs. Surratt's house. "Mark you," said McDevitt, "this was the first intimation given or received by anyone as to where the plot was hatched."[33]

Late on Monday evening, nearly two days after the police raid on Mrs. Surratt's, government agents descended on the house.[34] Major H. W. Smith, in charge of the party, rang the bell. Mrs. Surratt came to the window and asked, "Is that you, Mr. Kirby?"[35] Smith told her it was not Mr. Kirby and ordered her to open the door. As she opened the door, Smith asked if she were Mrs. Surratt and, when satisfied that she was, told her, "I come to arrest you and all in your house, and take you for examination to General Augur's headquarters."[36] The household was now one of women only, Weichmann and John Holahan having been working with the metropolitan police since Saturday morning. The women were gathered in the parlor when Captain R. C. Morgan arrived ten minutes later; they were sitting in silence, having been ordered not to talk to each other, while Mrs. Surratt gathered their wraps. Morgan and Captain Wermerskirch, another of the raiding party, heard a

[33] "Some Interesting Reminiscences of a Thrilling Night," Washington *Evening Star*, April 14, 1894.

[34] Why government agents took so long to find this establishment is puzzling since the newspapers announced the day after the murder that John Surratt "is said to be" the man who attacked the Secretary of State. Nor do we know why Major Smith was ordered to move when he was, thus belatedly.

[35] A neighbor of Mrs. Surratt's.

[36] Pitman, *The Trial*, 121.

knock at the door, and a man, dressed like a day laborer and carrying a pick, stood at the front door. The man said he had come to dig a gutter for Mrs. Surratt. The man was brought in just as the ladies of the household were passing out the door, Mrs. Surratt muttering a few words Captain Morgan did not catch.[37] The man was placed under arrest and sent off after the ladies to headquarters; the officers stayed, searching the house until three o'clock in the morning.

At General Augur's headquarters Mrs. Surratt was taken into an inner room and examined,[38] her companions staying outside. Only one incident occurred worthy of note. When the "laborer" was brought into the room after the ladies' arrival, someone suggested that this might be Miss Surratt's brother, and this so upset the young lady that Mrs. Surratt had to be called to calm her nervous, tearful daughter. When the improvised skullcap the "laborer" wore was removed, Miss Fitzpatrick for the first time recognized him as the man she had known as "Wood," a visitor at Mrs. Surratt's a few days in March.[39] This "Wood" was Payne, the man who had attacked the Secretary of State as Booth shot Lincoln.

Mrs. Surratt and her daughter and boarders were then

[37] Testimony of R. C. Morgan, *Restricted Material,* May 19; also Poore, *Conspiracy Trial,* II, 13–14. The controversy between this officer and his fellow officers over Mrs. Surratt's nonrecognition of Payne on this occasion will be detailed in subsequent chapters.

[38] This statement of Mrs. Surratt's remained in the hands of the War Department and was not released for nearly half a century. Writing in 1909, DeWitt said of this statement, "Its contents have never seen the light." *Assassination of Lincoln,* 66.

[39] Pitman, *The Trial,* 132.

taken to the Carroll Annex of the Old Capitol Prison.[40] We are fortunate in having a graphic account of the time she spent there, for one of her fellow inmates kept a diary which was published two years later. This woman, Virginia Lomax, relates what she was told of the Surratt affair by Miss Fitzpatrick. She describes Mrs. Surratt in prison and the conditions under which the prisoner lived—the poor food, the difficulty of getting fresh air, and so on.[41] Finally, she tells that, on a Sunday evening, the Old Capitol inmates were talking together when Mrs. Surratt was called for by a carriage and officers. Mrs. Surratt was taken away from her daughter and the prison, and, although those who were left sat up all night waiting for her return, they never saw Mrs. Surratt again. Miss Lomax relates also that a government agent (whom she designates only as "H") later told them that Mrs. Surratt was aboard a gunboat, confined in darkness and solitude, and that the government was thinking of sinking the gunboat with all the prisoners aboard.[42]

[40] The Old Capitol was a long, three-story building of dingy brick, erected to house Congress after the British had burned the Capitol in 1814. It was converted to a prison for political prisoners during the Civil War; at one time more than a thousand men were confined in its fifty-odd rooms. The building stood at the southeast corner of First and A streets, N.E., with a frame addition on the A Street side forming the Annex. The prison was closed in the summer of 1865, and the building underwent extensive remodeling in later years. It was torn down in 1930 to make way for the new Supreme Court building.

[41] Virginia Lomax, *The Old Capitol and Its Inmates*, 83, 87, 89, 136–37. A rare book, but quoted extensively in Eisenschiml, *In the Shadow of Lincoln's Death*, 113–16.

Mrs. Surratt's Tavern at Surrattsville

Courtesy National Park Service

The story that Mrs. Surratt was taken from the Old Capitol and placed on board one of the two government gunboats where the male prisoners were confined has no basis in fact other than the word of a detective whose only identity is "H." Yet the story has been repeated by nearly every writer on the Surratt case,[43] although it is possible to state definitely that she was never aboard a gunboat. In her narrative, Miss Lomax says Mrs. Surratt was removed from Old Capitol on a Sunday; it has been assumed that the Sunday in question was April 23.[44] Confirmation for this might seem to come from the fact that when Father Walter tried to reach Mrs. Surratt on April 25 at the Old Capitol, he was told she had been removed, though Walter added that he found she had been removed to "the Old Penitentiary" and made no mention of a gunboat.[45] However, we have a statement made in Carroll Prison by Mrs. Surratt on April 28 and, more to the point, a list[46] of all persons placed in

[42] Lomax, *op. cit.*, 175.

[43] David DeWitt, the most careful historian who has written of the case, does not make this error, but fails to mention anything in this connection at all.

[44] It has been assumed that the Lomax record refers to the week following Mrs. Surratt's arrest; hence the widespread belief that she was confined aboard a government gunboat. See Eisenschiml, *In the Shadow*, 113–17; Laughlin, *Death of Lincoln*, 163; George Bryan, *Great American Myth*, 273.

[45] Rev. J. A. Walter, *Church News* (Washington, D. C., August 16, 1891); paper read before the U.S. Catholic Historical Society, May 25, 1891.

[46] *Register of Prisoners*, Old Capitol, Military Department of the District of Columbia. Also, Colonel Baker to Colonel H. H. Wells, Archives, RG 153, JAO, Box 3, "R," 266.

the Old Capitol and its Carroll Annex in connection with the assassination, both of which indicate the Sunday in question was not April 23. This list shows Miss Lomax was not admitted until April 27. Thus Miss Lomax's record must cover the days between that date and her release on May 2; therefore, the Sunday to which she refers must have been Sunday the thirtieth of April, not Sunday the twenty-third. In addition, we have a little-known eyewitness account of Mrs. Surratt's being brought to the Old Penitentiary by Colonel Baker "an evening or so" after the landing of the male prisoners.[47] As the date of the landing of the male prisoners at the Old Penitentiary was reported in the newspapers of the period, it may definitely be given as April 29, at midnight.[48] Hence it is certain that Mrs. Surratt was never aboard a gunboat, many writers' opinions to the contrary notwithstanding.

Here a word must be said about the treatment Mrs. Surratt received. When first taken to the Old Penitentiary,[49] she was put into a common cell on the first floor (cell num-

[47] R. A. Watts, "The Trial and Execution of the Lincoln Conspirators," *Michigan History Magazine,* Vol. V (1922), 87. The writer is indebted to Colonel Julian E. Raymond, former post commander, Fort Lesley McNair, for calling his attention to this article, which has generally escaped notice.

[48] Washington *Evening Star,* July 7, 1865.

[49] The Old Penitentiary was authorized in 1826 for federal and local prisoners. It was situated on the Potomac at Greenleaf Point, in southwest Washington, and was a busy place during the Civil War when women worked at making munitions in the Arsenal while prisoners languished in tiny cells behind the grim brick walls of the penitentiary grounds. Renamed the Army War College in 1939, it became Fort Lesley McNair in 1946.

ber 153).[50] It was while she was here that Mrs. Surratt undoubtedly developed the illness from which she suffered until her death. One of her counsel later said that she was put in a cell two and one-half by eight feet, with a straw pallet and one bucket, and as she had what the counsel terms "the womb disease," she "flooded for three weeks until removed by additional medical advice, but too late to stop the flooding which went on until she died." The lawyer believed Mrs. Surratt was mortally ill at the time she was hanged.[51]

William E. Doster, former provost marshal of the District of Columbia, who undertook the defense of Atzerodt and Payne, wrote, "Mrs. Surratt was sick during a great part of her trial. . . . Her sickness was change of life, which weakened her greatly. Her cell by reason of her sickness was scarcely habitable." And he adds, "I doubt whether she knew much of her execution. She behaved as one that was three-fourths dead."[52]

Mrs. Surratt's treatment was harsh, but it was no worse than that given other political prisoners in the Old Penitentiary at the time.[53] And she fared better than the male prisoners held in connection with the assassination, for she

[50] Washington *Daily Morning Chronicle,* July 8, 1865.

[51] Frederick W. Aiken to G. A. Townsend, in "The Widow Surratt," unidentified newspaper clipping.

[52] William E. Doster, *Lincoln and Episodes of the Civil War,* 276.

[53] Jefferson Davis' secretary, Burton Harrison, was in the penitentiary when Mrs. Surratt was confined there. He was put into a cell four feet by eight, "dark as night in the daytime," and for furniture he had a blanket on the cement floor. See Mrs. Burton Harrison's *Recollections—Grave and Gay,* 232.

was never hooded as they were.[54] Nor does Secretary of War Stanton seem to have been especially vindictive toward the woman prisoner. A report made by Dr. John T. Gray, dated June 20, reveals that none of the prisoners had yet been supplied with anything to sit on but a hair pillow—the doctor recommended the men be given a box or stool and that Mrs. Surratt be supplied with a chair.[55] Dr. Gray's examination was made at Stanton's request, and, in a letter to General Hancock (who was in charge of the penitentiary), the Secretary authorized Hancock to do anything for Mrs. Surratt's comfort "consistent with her secure detention," and "to allow her to be furnished with any food or necessaries she may desire. . . . Such changes or additions to her furniture as may add to her comfort are also authorized."[56]

Eventually Mrs. Surratt was removed to a large cell on the third floor,[57] and there she enjoyed many extra privileges, especially after the close of her trial. R. A. Watts, assistant adjutant general and close associate of General

[54] Samuel Arnold was later to describe vividly these padded hoods (and his own damp, unfurnished penitentiary cell) in a series of articles in the Baltimore *American* in 1902. They have been described often and must have been quite painful, especially as the Washington summer drew on.

[55] Report of Dr. John T. Gray to Stanton, Stanton Papers, XXVII, Library of Congress, Manuscript Division. Dr. Gray, who was head of the Utica infirmary, urged Stanton to remove the hoods the male prisoners wore lest they go insane.

[56] Draft of a letter from Stanton to Hancock, Stanton Papers, XXVII, Library of Congress. Letter dated June 19, 1865.

[57] Washington *Daily Morning Chronicle*, July 8; Washington *Evening Star*, July 7.

Hancock, reports that "during much of the time she occupied a large, airy room on the third floor, and her daughter Anna was frequently permitted to be with her."[58] Captain Christian Rath, the hangman, reports Anna a daily visitor to the prison, taking her meals with her mother often, staying nearly all day after the trial.[59] A skeptic might doubt these sources, as they are governmental. Perhaps the most convincing evidence is the testimony by Henry Kyd Douglas, also a political prisoner at the penitentiary, who was lucky enough to be given "a comfortable room" next to Mrs. Surratt's; as his room was next to the courtroom, it must have been on the third floor of the penitentiary. In addition, Douglas says, "Mrs. Surratt . . . was supposed to be fed on prisoners' rations, like the others, but in fact, Hartranft sent her daily from his table not only the substantials but the delicacies with which it was so abundantly supplied."[60]

Whether Mrs. Surratt was ironed or not is more difficult to determine. Douglas says she was not, "although so represented in the pictorial papers."[61] Her counsel, Frederick Aiken, in a letter to the Washington *Chronicle,* said she "was at no time ironed in the presence of the court."[62] On the other hand, all of the newspapers reported her ironed at the time of the trial. Ben Poore, editor of the Boston

[58] Watts, *loc. cit.,* 88.

[59] John A. Gray, "Fate of the Lincoln Conspirators," *McClures,* Vol. LXXXII (October, 1911), 634.

[60] Henry Kyd Douglas, *I Rode With Stonewall,* 340, 344. Gen. Hartranft was responsible for the secure detention of the prisoners.

[61] *Ibid.,* 344.

[62] Washington *Daily Morning Chronicle,* September 19, 1873.

record of the trial testimony, said she was ironed.[63] Edward V. Murphy, one of the official reporters, wrote many years later, "For the first few days of the trial Mrs. Surratt was brought into the courtroom with an iron ball and chain fastened to her ankle and with her hands manacled. The manacles were later removed, because of the comments of the press."[64] Frederick Stone, one of the defense attorneys, once visited her in her cell and recalled, "She was ironed, but not heavily, like the others."[65] And so eyewitnesses contradict each other. On the whole, it seems probable she was ironed when first put into the Old Penitentiary, but that the irons were removed as the trial went on and as her health failed.[66]

Before going on to Mrs. Surratt's fortunes at the conspiracy trial, we must go back a little in our story. To understand the nature, methods, and setting of the trial, it is important to recall the mood, temper, and trend of the times in which it took place. To give this background, it is necessary to return to the central event of the whole story, the night of April 14, when John Wilkes Booth shot the President.

[63] *Conspiracy Trial,* I, Introduction, 11.
[64] *New York Times Magazine,* April 9, 1916.
[65] *New York Tribune,* interview, April 17, 1883.
[66] Compare Eisenschiml's conclusions, *In the Shadow,* 124.

CHAPTER II

Mrs. Surratt's First Trial

WASHINGTON was changed by the assassination from a riotously bedecked and celebrating city to a city of mourning. The reaction must have been as terrific as it was sudden and unexpected. The *National Intelligencer* reported on the morning of April 15: "Such a night of horror has seldom darkened any community. The indefinite dread which conspiracy inspires seized on the public mind, and suspicion, apprehension, and agony pervaded the people." Men, not knowing truth from rumor, were uneasy, restless, and inclined to violence. A mob rushed a man to a lamppost to be hanged because he had expressed pleasure at Lincoln's death.[1] And the *Star* spoke of "the terrible act committed by the conquered South yesterday, through its representative, the assassin. . . ." It was believed that the assassination was the last effort of the dying Confederacy.[2]

[1] Judge I. G. Kimball, *Recollections*, 70–71.

[2] James Ford Rhodes has written that magnanimity to the beaten foe was the sentiment on Monday before the assassination;

The spontaneous reaction of the people of the North can be gauged from the nature of expressions of sympathy which poured into Washington from dozens of cities and citizens' clubs. The Albany, New York, Y.M.C.A. board of directors saw in the assassin's attack "the legitimate fruit of that treason whose seed was planted in secession."[3] The German Citizens of Boston thought, on April 20, that the crime "must be traced in its origin and object to the rebel chief Jefferson Davis."[4] The trustees of Columbia College in New York, on April 17, identified the cause of human bondage, the starvation of prisoners of war, and other outrages with the cause "which finally sends into the heart of our populous towns . . . the midnight incendiary with his torch and the dastardly assassin with his knife."[5] The Athenaeum Club, meeting April 19, said the rebellion, "which began in the blackest treachery," was ended "in the foulest assassination."[6] These were the sentiments of the Northern people as shown in the resolutions adopted by groups of citizens through their social organizations. These resolutions illustrate vividly the emotion and vengeance of the times.

It was within the power of the government in Washing-

a cry for justice and vengeance and a demand that the Rebellion leaders be hanged was heard everywhere on the Saturday following the assassination. The contemporary record bears out this judgment completely. Rhodes, *History of the United States*, V, 148.

[3] *The Assassination of President Lincoln*, Expressions of Condolence and Sympathy, 652. These "expressions" were assembled and published by the Department of State.

[4] *Ibid.*, 657.

[5] *Ibid.*, 676.

[6] *Ibid.*, 686.

ton to try to allay this spirit of revenge upon the beaten South. But information reaching the War Department and its Bureau of Military Justice was not of a nature to calm suspicion or to lead the government to take a charitable view of things. When Booth's room at the National Hotel was searched, a letter was found in his trunk which, among other things, advised a consultation with Richmond before further action be taken by the plotters.[7] Probably on the strength of this letter, Detective B. A. Hill told Stanton on April 16 that "all the circumstances signify a plot laid at Richmond before the capture of that city. I regret to think so, but it must be so."[8] After the assassination a flood of statements, rumors, and reports inundated the War Department, and, by the second of May, the government felt sure enough of its case for the President to issue a proclamation which asserted that "it appears from evidence in the Bureau of Military Justice that the atrocious murder of . . . Abraham Lincoln and the attempted assassination of William H. Seward . . . were incited, concerted, and procured by and between Jefferson Davis, late of Richmond, and Jacob Thompson, Clement C. Clay," and others of the so-called Canadian Cabinet.[9]

It was in this atmosphere that the trial of Booth's ac-

[7] This letter was to Booth from Samuel Arnold. Arnold explained he had withdrawn from the "enterprise," advised Booth to be cautious, and said, "I would prefer your first query 'Go and see how it will be taken in R——d.' " Poore, *Conspiracy Trial,* I, 420.

[8] Hill to Stanton, Stanton Papers, XXV, Library of Congress, Manuscript Division.

[9] *War of the Rebellion, Official Records of the Union and Confederate Armies,* Series I, Vol. XLIX, Part II, 566–67 (hereinafter cited as OR).

complices and alleged accomplices proceeded. Secretary of War Stanton obtained an opinion from Attorney General Speed to enable a special military commission to try the accused. The civil courts were open, and Gideon Welles, secretary of the navy, regretted that the trial was not to be in civil court; but Stanton "was emphatic" on that point, though Welles thought Speed at first "otherwise inclined."[10] On the first of May the President ordered that nine competent judges be selected, and five days later these were detailed. The judges who made up the court were as follows: two major generals, David Hunter and Lewis Wallace; a brevet major general, August V. Kautz; three brigadier generals, Albion Howe, R. S. Foster, and Thomas M. Harris; a brevet brigadier general, James A. Ekin; a brevet colonel, Charles H. Tompkins; and a lieutenant colonel, David Clendenin.[11] A courtroom was arranged in a large room of the Old Penitentiary.[12]

[10] Gideon Welles, *Diary*, II, 303.

[11] Pitman, *The Trial*, 18.

[12] The courtroom was the northeast corner room of the third floor of the east wing of the Old Penitentiary. It was about thirty feet by forty, was whitewashed and furnished with carpets, tables, and chairs especially for the trial. Three wooden pillars eleven feet high supported the ceiling. There were four windows, heavily grated, two on the north side, two on the east. Contemporary sources describe the room and the penitentiary minutely.

But what is not generally known is that not all of the Old Penitentiary was torn down in later rebuilding and refurbishing, although that is widely believed. "Every account—and there are many—says something to this effect," wrote Colonel Julian E. Raymond in his "History of Fort Lesley McNair" (manuscript), 83. In fact, the old east wing of the penitentiary still stands, and the northeast corner room, where the trial was held, can still be found.

On May 10 the court assembled, and the charge and specification against the prisoners were read. At this session the commission adopted eleven rules of procedure by which it would govern itself. On May 12 the taking of testimony began, with testimony for the prosecution closing May 23, a total of 131 witnesses having been examined. Defense testimony followed, and the summing up of the counsel began June 16. On June 29 and 30 the commission deliberated on the evidence, and its verdicts were announced on July 5, after the President had approved the findings.

It should be noted here that the government had not escaped criticism for convening this commission. It was announced on May 9 that no reporters would be admitted to the trial and that the testimony and progress of the trial would not be made public.[13] The New York newspapers denounced these proceedings as unconstitutional. The New York *World* wrote of the "Military Star Chamber" in Washington, protesting that the civil courts were open; the *World* was joined by Horace Greeley's *Tribune*, the *Times*, and the *Evening Post*. Every paper except the *Herald* expressed regret at the conduct of the trial. Attorney General Speed's predecessor, Edward Bates, addressed the people

Though completely remodeled inside, the windows and chimneys of the courtroom are plainly visible. About a foot of brick facing has been added to the outside wall of the building, and, of course, the gratings are gone from the windows, but otherwise the exterior is the same as it was in 1865. The building is now converted to officers' quarters.

The writer is indebted to Colonel Raymond, who was until recently post commander at Fort Lesley McNair, for information concerning the penitentiary as it was and as it is today.

[13] Washington *Evening Star*, May 9, 1865.

of Missouri, declaring that "every American who is not an extreme radical must know" that the law is sovereign, and who tramples upon it "cannot possibly be a loyal man."[14] The Washington *Star*, as a friend of the Administration, felt called upon to defend the trial from the attacks of these "and other extremist journals."[15]

The upshot of all this criticism was that on May 13 the court was opened to newspaper reporters. Editorially the *World* expressed its satisfaction that "something is accomplished for the national honor and law," but concluded that "the greater wrong remains," as the civil courts were "still to be superseded."[16] The *Tribune* congratulated the government on this decision.[17]

But the day the press was admitted to the courtroom, the court heard in secret ("for prudential reasons") the testimony of Sanford Conover, Richard Montgomery, and James Merritt.[18] It was chiefly upon the evidence given by these three that the Bureau of Military Justice rested its case against the Confederacy. In a consideration of the conspiracy trial it does not matter that a year later this testimony was found to be a tissue of lies or that Conover was

[14] Quoted in the New York *World*, May 6, 1865. Bates wrote in his *Diary*, May 25, "I am pained to be led to believe that my successor, Attorney General Speed, has been wheedled out of an *opinion*, to the effect that such a trial is lawful. If he be, in the lowest degree, qualified for his office, he must know better." Bates, *Diary*, 483.

[15] *Evening Star*, May 13, 1865.

[16] New York *World*, May 15, 1865.

[17] New York *Tribune*, May 15, 1865.

[18] Pitman, *The Trial*, 21 (footnote). This evidence was released June 5.

convicted for perjury and sentenced to ten years at Albany Penitentiary.[19] The important thing is that this evidence was accepted unquestioningly in 1865 and was felt by those in authority to prove Southern complicity in the assassination. Southern leaders were specifically charged with complicity at this trial and were tried *in absentia.*[20]

The difficulties under which the defense labored arose from two sources: the denial of certain rights of the accused, and the state of criminal law in 1865.

Thomas Ewing, in his argument against the jurisdiction of the military commission on June 23, 1865, spelled out some of the rights which were being denied the accused at that trial. He protested that the prisoners could not be compelled to answer the accusation of several crimes in one count after the act of Congress of February 26, 1853, Section 117.[21] He pointed out that if the crime of the accused approached treason, the accused were to have a copy of the indictment and a list of the jury and of all the witnesses to be used to prove the said indictment three days before they were to be tried—under the act of April 30, 1790, Section 24, page 221.[22] Reverdy Johnson had already indicated

[19] The House Judiciary Committee exposed Conover in July, 1866. See *House Report No. 104*, 39 Cong., 1 sess.

[20] Judge Advocate Holt appeared before this House committee and, after its disclosures, disowned Conover, whom he asserted had duped him (Holt to Stanton, *OR*, II, 8, 945). But Judge Holt still believed in the complicity of Jefferson Davis and other Confederate leaders, even after Conover's testimony was discredited. See Holt's *Vindication* (first published September 3, 1866, reprinted later as a pamphlet).

[21] Pitman, *The Trial*, 265.

[22] *Ibid.*, 265. The accused did not hear the charge against them until the opening day of the trial.

that the prisoners should not be kept in the dock in chains (as they were, with the possible exception of Mrs. Surratt).

Ewing also hit at a feature of martial law as it was in 1865; the joint duties of the judge advocate made him prosecutor and judge at a military trial. Ewing remarked that the judge advocate had received the reports of detectives, pre-examined the witnesses, prepared and signed the charges, and that he controlled the admission and rejection of the evidence before the court. Yet, in a civil court, a judge who had heard the client's story could not sit on the trial lest he be partial.[23]

In this connection it should be noted that writers on this trial have often remarked that the accused were not permitted to testify in their own behalf. This is true. But the partisans of Mrs. Surratt who have asserted that had she been tried in civil court she could have been heard have overshot the mark. She could have been heard only if she had been tried in the civil criminal courts of one state in the Union—Maine.[24] For the right to testify in one's own behalf is not a right based upon English common law,[25] and it was first guaranteed in the federal courts, in all United States courts, in territorial courts, and in courts-martial by

[23] *Ibid.*, 266.

[24] Maine was the first state to permit the defendant in criminal cases to testify in his own behalf, in 1864. Massachusetts granted the right in 1866; Connecticut, in 1867; New York and New Hampshire, in 1869; New Jersey, in 1871. See J. B. Thayer, *Cases on Evidence*, 1117; Charles Warren, *A History of the American Bar*, 473; J. H. Wigmore, *Wigmore on Evidence*, II, Section 579, 701 ff.

[25] *Two Centuries Growth of American Law*, 1701–1901, 340.

the act of Congress of March 16, 1878.[26] Until that time courts-martial and military commissions followed the rules of evidence of common law as reflected in the criminal courts of the country.[27] Thus, in this particular, the ruling of the commission was not in any way vindictive or (legally) unduly harsh.

According to one of the lawyers, William Doster, the prisoners were not permitted to talk with their counsel except in the courtroom, in whispers, with a crowd around them.[28] This statement must be qualified, however, for Doster saw Payne alone when Payne requested it,[29] Frederick Stone visited Mrs. Surratt in her cell,[30] and Thomas Ewing visited Samuel Arnold in his cell.[31] Stone said, "The rule . . . was that the prisoners should see their counsel in the presence of a guard but not necessarily in the hearing thereof."[32] The ruling here, it may be said in the government's defense, does not appear to have been extreme.

The charge against the prisoners read that the accused had "maliciously, unlawfully, and traitorously" conspired

[26] U.S.C., 1946 edition, Title 28 Sec. 632 (act of March 16, 1878, 20 Stat. 30).

[27] Colonel W. W. Winthrop, *Military Law,* I, 50–51. Also Winthrop, *Military Law and Precedents,* 313. Also Wigmore, *op. cit.,* I, Section d, 99–100.

[28] Doster, *op. cit.,* 260.

[29] *Ibid.,* 265.

[30] Frederick Stone in New York *Tribune* interview, April 17, 1883.

[31] Samuel Arnold, "The Lincoln Plot," *Baltimore American,* 1902. (In Lincoln clippings, Washingtoniana Division, Washington, D. C. Public Library.)

[32] Stone, *loc. cit.*

with John H. Surratt, John Wilkes Booth, Jefferson Davis, and other Confederate leaders to kill and murder President Lincoln, Vice-President Johnson, Secretary of State Seward, and General U. S. Grant.[33] Thus worded, the charge was indefinable by any known rules of war, coming only under the head of what the Judge Advocate called the "common law of war," and, in addition, was sufficiently vague to permit no distinction to be made between the plot to kidnap Lincoln and the plot to take his life.[34]

It is not the writer's intention to tell the whole story of this trial. Our concern here is with Mrs. Surratt, and the background of the trial and the atmosphere in which it proceeded are important only insofar as they set the stage for a consideration of the evidence against this woman. But the fact that she was a Southern woman on trial before a jury of Union generals and that these jurymen had every reason to believe that her son was as deep in the murder plot as the assassin himself is of some consequence here.

The charge against Mrs. Surratt was the one against them all and has been considered. The specification against the woman read:

> And in further prosecution of said conspiracy, Mary E. Surratt did, at Washington City, and within the military department and military lines aforesaid, on or before the 6th day of March, A.D. 1865, and on divers other days and times between that day and the 20th day of April, A. D. 1865, receive,

[33] Pitman, *The Trial,* 18–19.

[34] Ewing tried in vain to get a definition of this term "common law of war," and in vain pointed out that it was "a term unknown—*a quiddity*—undefined and incapable of definition." *Ibid.,* 318.

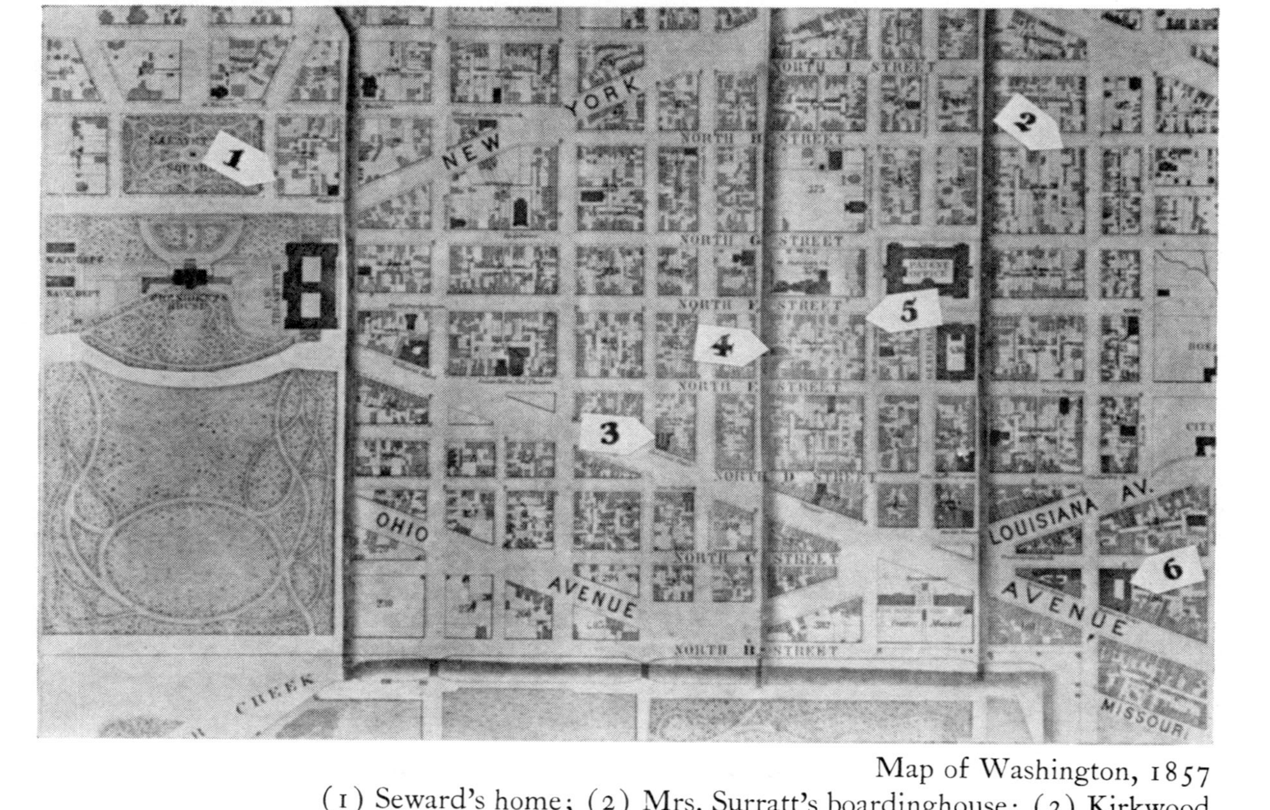

Map of Washington, 1857
(1) Seward's home; (2) Mrs. Surratt's boardinghouse; (3) Kirkwood House; (4) Site of Ford's Theater; (5) Herndon House; (6) National Hotel *Library of Congress, Map Division*

entertain, harbor, and conceal, aid and assist the said John Wilkes Booth, David E. Herold, Lewis Payne, John H. Surratt, Michael O'Laughlin, George A. Atzerodt, and Samuel Arnold and their confederates, with the knowledge of the murderous and traitorous conspiracy aforesaid and with the intent to aid, abet and assist them in the execution thereof, and in escaping from justice after the murder of the said Abraham Lincoln, in persuance of said conspiracy in manner aforesaid.[35]

Defending Mrs. Surratt were two young men, Frederick Aiken, graduate of the Howard law school (not to be confused with the present Howard University), and John W. Clampitt, graduate of Columbian College (now George Washington University). Most important of Mrs. Surratt's legal aides was Reverdy Johnson, the distinguished Maryland senator, who came forward his first day in court to argue ably that a military court had no right to sit in the cases of the accused, but that the prisoners should be tried in the regular criminal courts, which were open.

When Reverdy Johnson appeared in court, General Harris objected to his admission on the ground that Johnson did not recognize the moral obligation of an oath designed as a test of loyalty. By this simple objection General Harris successfully deprived Mrs. Surratt of her most able defender, for Johnson's position was made suspect in the eyes of the court, and he appeared only twice more throughout the balance of the trial. In the opinion of two of the other defense attorneys, Johnson's withdrawal was prejudicial to his client.[36]

[35] Pitman, *The Trial*, 20.

[36] Doster thought many drew the conclusion that Johnson had

What of the case against Mrs. Surratt?

To begin with, circumstantial evidence was against her. After she moved to Washington in October, 1864, several of the conspirators had boarded at her H Street house—though Booth had not, and those who had stayed there were transient. Still, it was generally believed that, in President Johnson's phrase, "she kept the nest that hatched the egg." The chief witnesses against her were John M. Lloyd, who kept her Surrattsville tavern, and Louis Weichmann, who boarded with her in Washington.

It is indicative of the spirit in which she was tried that no better statement of the case against Mrs. Surratt can be made than that made at the close of her trial by the Assistant Judge Advocate John A. Bingham—a man who, under military law, should have presented an unbiased review of the evidence. Bingham, arguing for two days, on June 27 and 28, stressed the main points in the testimony against Mrs. Surratt.

Devoting nearly one-half of his address to the charge made by Reverdy Johnson challenging the right of the military court to sit on this trial, Bingham restated Johnson's proposition in these words:

---

given up her case. (Doster, *op. cit.*, 264.) Frederick Stone said that Mrs. Surratt asked him to take her case during the trial, as she felt she was being sacrificed by the incapacity of her counsel; Stone particularly censures Reverdy Johnson, saying, "He came forward and made an argument against the jurisdiction of the military court, to be read and applauded by the people, and then abandoned the woman." Stone, *loc. cit.* However, Johnson continued to work with Aiken and Clampitt and probably withdrew from the courtroom because he felt his appearance would do her more harm than good.

That Congress has not authorized, and, under the Constitution cannot authorize the appointment of this Commission.

That this Commission has "as a court, no legal existence or authority," because the President, who alone appointed the Commission has no such power.

That his act "is a mere nullity—the usurpation of a power not vested in the executive, and conferring no authority upon you."[37]

Bingham replied that military commissions were authorized under martial law and that martial law was declared throughout the United States by a competent authority, Lincoln, in his proclamation of September 24, 1862.[38]

Bingham cited the Congressional act of March 3, 1863, which authorized the President to suspend the writ of habeas corpus, and which ordered that "all rebels, insurgents, their aiders and abettors, and persons guilty of any disloyal practice affording aid and comfort to rebels . . . should be subject to martial law and liable to trial and punishment by a military commission."[39]

Then, after reviewing the case against the Confederacy,[40] Bingham came to a consideration of Mrs. Surratt. Of her Bingham had this to say: "That Mary E. Surratt is as guilty as her son of having thus conspired, combined, and confederated to do this murder, in aid of this rebellion, is clear." Her house was the headquarters of Booth, John Surratt, Atzerodt, Payne, and Herold. She was inquired

[37] Pitman, *The Trial*, 353.

[38] *Ibid.*, 359

[39] *Ibid.*, 369.

[40] *Ibid.*, 373–80.

for by Payne, visited by Booth, and held private conversations with him. Booth's picture, "together with that of the chief conspirator, Jefferson Davis," was found at her home. On the eleventh of April she sent to Booth for a carriage to go to Surrattsville, and he, having disposed of his carriage, gave her agent ten dollars to hire one. "The pretense is made" that Mrs. Surratt was going to Surrattsville on her lawful, private business, but "can anyone tell, if this be so, how it comes that she should apply to Booth for a conveyance, and how it comes that he, of his own accord . . . should send her ten dollars with which to procure it?" He was under no obligation to her.[41]

On her trip to Surrattsville on the eleventh, Bingham recalled, Mrs. Surratt met John M. Lloyd at Uniontown.[42] She called to him; he got out of his carriage and came to her, and she whispered to him in so low a tone her attendant could not hear; though Lloyd distinctly heard and testified she had told him to have those "shooting irons" ready, meaning the carbines her son had left with Lloyd, adding that "they would soon be called for."[43]

On April 14, Mrs. Surratt sent for Booth, had an interview with him in her house, and immediately went to Surrattsville. She delivered to Lloyd a field glass at about six that afternoon and told him "to have two bottles of whiskey and the carbines ready, as they would be called for that night." Mrs. Surratt could not have known that the arms would be called for and what route the assassins would take

[41] *Ibid.*, 392.

[42] Now Anacostia; it lies just across the Anacostia River, within the District of Columbia.

[43] Pitman, *The Trial*, 392.

in their flight had she not been in on the conspiracy, Bingham said.

Was Lloyd in on this conspiracy? The Assistant Judge Advocate explained:

> The explanation is that he was dependent upon Mary E. Surratt; was her tenant; and his declaration, given in evidence by the accused himself, is that "she has ruined him, and brought this trouble upon him." But because he was weak enough, or wicked enough, to become the guilty depository of these arms and to deliver them on the order of Mary E. Surratt to the assassins, it does not follow that he is not to be believed under oath. . . . Is he not corroborated in the fact of the first interview with Mrs. Surratt by the joint testimony of Mrs. Offut and Louis J. Weichmann, each of whom testified (and they are contradicted by no one), that on Tuesday, the 11th of April, at Uniontown, Mrs. Surratt called Mr. Lloyd to come to her, which he did, and she held a *secret* conversation with him? Is he not corroborated as to the last conversation on the 14th of April by the testimony of Mrs. Offut, who swears that upon the evening of the 14th of April she saw the prisoner, Mary E. Surratt, at Lloyd's house, approach and hold conversation with him? Is he not corroborated in the fact, to which he swears, that Mrs. Surratt delivered to him at that time the fieldglass wrapped in paper, by the sworn statement of Weichmann that Mrs. Surratt took with her on that occasion two packages, both of which were wrapped in paper, and one of which he describes as a small package about six inches in diameter? The attempt was made by calling Mrs. Offut to prove that no such package was delivered, but it failed; she merely states that Mrs. Surratt delivered a package wrapped in paper to her after her arrival there, and before Lloyd came in, which was laid down in the room. But whether it was *the* package about which Lloyd testi-

fies, or the other package of the two about which Weichmann testifies, as having been carried there that day by Mrs. Surratt, does not appear. Neither does this witness pretend to say that Mrs. Surratt, after she had delivered it to her, and the witness had laid it down in the room, did not again take it up, if it were the same, and put it in the hands of Lloyd. She only knows that she did not see that done; but she did see Lloyd with a package like the one she received in the room before Mrs. Surratt left. How it came into his possession she is not able to state; nor what the package was that Mrs. Surratt first handed her; nor which of the packages it was she afterwards saw in the hands of Lloyd.

But there is one other fact in this case that puts forever at rest the question of the guilty participation of the prisoner Mrs. Surratt in this conspiracy and murder; and that is that Payne, who had lodged for four days in her house, who, during all that time had sat at her table, and who had often conversed with her, when the guilt of his great crime was upon him, and he knew not where else he could so safely go to find a co-conspirator, and he could trust none that was not like himself, guilty, with even the knowledge of his presence, under cover of darkness, after wandering for three days and nights, skulking before the pursuing officers of justice, at the hour of midnight, found his way to the door of Mrs. Surratt, rang the bell, was admitted, and upon being asked, "Whom do you want to see?" replied, "Mrs. Surratt." He was then asked by the officer Morgan, what he came at that time of night for, to which he replied "to dig a gutter in the morning; Mrs. Surratt had sent for him." Being asked where he last worked, he replied "sometimes on 'I' Street," and where he boarded, he replied, "he had no boarding house, and was a poor man who got his living with the pick," which he bore upon his shoulder, having stolen it from the intrenchments of the capital. Upon being pressed again why he came there at that time of night to go to work, he answered that he simply called to see what time he should go to work in the morning. Upon being told by the officer who fortunately had preceded him to this house that he would have to go to the provost marshall's office, he moved and did not answer, whereupon Mrs. Surratt was asked to step into the hall and state whether she knew this man. Raising her right hand she exclaimed, "Before God, Sir, I have not seen that man before; I have not hired him; I do not know anything about him." The hall was brilliantly lighted.

If not one word had been said, the mere act of Payne in flying to her house for shelter would have borne witness against her, strong as proofs of Holy Writ. But when she denies, after hearing his declaration that she had sent for him, or that she had gone to him and hired him, and calls for God to witness that she had never seen him, and knew nothing of him, when, in point of fact, she had seen him for four successive days in her own house, in the same clothing which he then wore, who can resist for a moment the conclusion that these parties were alike guilty?[44]

Frederick Aiken made the statement for Mrs. Surratt's defense.[45] After some preliminary remarks Aiken got down to points. Of her acquaintance with Booth, he said that, if the testimony was reliable, it began in the latter part of January, about three months before the assassination;[46] that when Booth called at her home, he asked for John H. Sur-

[44] *Ibid.*, 393–94.

[45] For Reverdy Johnson's comment, see p. 54.

[46] The actual date was January 1. This error arose because Weichmann swore throughout the trial that the street meeting of Booth, Mudd, Surratt, and himself took place January 15, instead of the correct date, December 23, 1864.

ratt (by Weichmann's testimony); and that it was John H. Surratt who asked Lloyd to hide the carbines for him (by Lloyd's testimony).[47]

Aiken said that after the testimony of Misses Surratt and Fitzpatrick was heard, there was no doubt that the photographs of Booth, Jefferson Davis, and others did not belong to Mrs. Surratt. Three circumstances constituted the part played by Mrs. Surratt in the conspiracy: her acquaintance with Booth, the messages to Lloyd on the eleventh and the fourteenth of April, and her declaration that she did not recognize Payne on the night of April 17.[48] Here Aiken undertook to examine Weichmann's testimony. Weichmann took board and lodging at Mrs. Surratt's on November 1, 1864; Payne spent the night in Weichmann's room (at Weichmann's request) on the occasion of his first visit at the rooming house, six weeks before the assassination. Three weeks later Payne returned and stayed about three days, again rooming with Weichmann. On this second visit, Weichmann testified, he found a false moustache on a table in his room. Weichmann took the moustache and locked it up in his trunk, but didn't say anything to Mrs. Surratt about it. On the same day, Weichmann went to John Surratt's room and found him seated on the bed with Payne, surrounded with revolvers and spurs and playing with bowie knives—but still Weichmann said nothing to Mrs. Surratt of these suspicious acts.[49]

In addition, Aiken pointed to Weichmann's intimate knowledge of John Surratt's movements between Rich-

[47] Pitman, *The Trial*, 292.

[48] *Ibid.*, 292.

[49] *Ibid.*, 294.

mond and Washington and his ability to fix the dates with great exactitude. Aiken noted that when John Surratt left Washington on April 3, he spent his last moments with Weichmann and told Weichmann of having had interviews with Jefferson Davis and others in Richmond.

Aiken pointed out that Weichmann swore that on April 2 he found the actor, John McCullough, in Booth's room, but that, according to McCullough's sworn statement, he (McCullough) was not in Washington after March 26. Aiken concluded, "One thing is apparent to our minds . . . that in order to have gained all this knowledge Weichmann must have been within the inner circle of the conspiracy. He knows too much for an innocent man."

Too, when Weichmann went to Booth on the eleventh to borrow his buggy, he was not asked by Mrs. Surratt to get ten dollars; it was offered by Booth to Weichmann. Booth was only an acquaintance of Mrs. Surratt's. Only intimacy would have excused Mrs. Surratt in accepting the favor, had she known about it, Aiken went on.[50] Even more damning, he concluded, was the telegram which Weichmann admitted was genuine:

> New York, March 23d, 1865—To Weichmann, Esq.,
> 541 H Street:
> Tell John telegraph number and street at once.
> (signed) J. Booth

"What additional proof of confidential relations between Weichmann and Booth could the Court desire?" Aiken asked. And he argued that if Weichmann had entire knowledge of the conspiracy, he would have known Mrs.

[50] *Ibid.*, 295.

Surratt's part and could produce evidence "in comparison with which all present facts of accusation would sink into insignificance."[51]

Aiken then proceeded to Lloyd's testimony that Mrs. Surratt told him to have the "shooting irons" (the carbines Lloyd had hidden for John Surratt some six weeks earlier) ready, on April 11. The testimony was as follows:

I am *quite positive* she asked me about the "shooting irons;" I am quite positive about that, but not altogether positive; I think she named shooting irons or something to call my attention to those things, for I had almost forgotten about their being there. Q. "Was her question to you first, whether they were there, or what was it?" A. "Really, I cannot recollect the first question put to me—I could not do it to save my life." The question was asked Lloyd, "During this conversation was the word carbine mentioned?" He answered, "No." "She finally came out, but I cannot be determined about it—that she said shooting irons—asked me in relation to them." The question was then asked, "Can you swear, on your oath, that Mrs. Surratt mentioned the words 'shooting irons' to you at all?" A. "I am very positive she did." Q. "Are you certain?" A. "I am very positive that she named shooting irons on both occasions. Not so positive as to the first as I am about the last."

Thus, argued Aiken, Lloyd cannot be too sure about the matter on his meeting Mrs. Surratt on the eleventh, but he can be definite that she did mention the subject of the "shooting irons" when he talked to her on the fourteenth. Yet, on the fourteenth, Lloyd was "more than ordinarily affected with intoxicating drink," by the testimony of

[51] *Ibid.*, 296.

his sister-in-law, Captain Gwynn, the barkeeper, and others. But Lloyd was presumably sober on the eleventh! Too, on April 11, when Lloyd said Mrs. Surratt asked him about the weapons, Weichmann, who was sitting in the buggy on the same seat with Mrs. Surratt, swore he heard nothing about the "shooting irons." Aiken asked, "Would not the quick ears of Weichmann have heard the remark had it been made? . . . All the facts connecting Lloyd with the case tend to his implication and guilt, and to prove that he adopted the *dernier ressort* of guilt—accusation and inculpation of another."[52]

Mrs. Surratt went to Surrattsville on April 14 solely to transact private business, Aiken said; a letter from Mr. Calvert in that connection was received by her before she saw Booth that day, or even before Booth knew that the President was going to the theater that night. Had Mrs. Surratt left a few minutes earlier, she wouldn't have seen the actor at all; at Surrattsville she was ready to leave when Lloyd drove up to the house—and she had not seen him. "All these things," Aiken concluded, "furnish powerful presumptions in favor of the theory that, if she delivered the messages at all, it was done innocently."

In regard to the nonrecognition of Payne, the last of the three major counts against Mrs. Surratt, Aiken pointed out that Mrs. Surratt's eyesight had been shown to be defective by the testimony of her daughter, Anna, Emma Offutt (Lloyd's sister-in-law), Eliza Holahan, Honora Fitzpatrick, and others. Then, too, she would have been nervous the night of the arrest, having just been aroused from bed. The man she had previously known as a Baptist

[52] *Ibid.*, 296.

parson was in the garb of an uncouthly dressed ditch digger. And of the two officers who gave testimony, one said the hall was brilliantly lighted, the other that the gaslight was purposely dimmed.[53]

This concluded Mr. Aiken's defense statement.

An examination of the evidence taken at the trial becomes highly desirable. It is available in the official record edited by Pitman; in Ben Poore's edition of two (sometimes three) volumes; in the pages of the Washington *National Intelligencer*, which published the entire proceedings; and in the restricted stenographic reports made by the official court reporters, still to be found in the war records of the Judge Advocate General in the National Archives in Washington. The Pitman record is endorsed by one of the special judge advocates of the trial, Colonel H. L. Burnett, who certified to its "faithfulness and accuracy"; and of the record Pitman himself asserted, "The entire testimony adduced at the trial of the assassins . . . is contained in the following pages. . . ."[54] Yet Pitman merely abridged the testimony, and no abridgment of testimony in this case can be wholly satisfactory. Poore's volumes and the *Intelligencer* give the full testimony,[55] and these transcripts agree with the restricted reports when a comparison is made. Thus, we can learn what the witnesses at the trial actually said, but it is no small task to do so.

A careful examination of the testimony for and against Mrs. Surratt reveals the following facts.

[53] *Ibid.*, 297.

[54] *Ibid.*, 1.

[55] The Poore record breaks off without explanation in the middle of testimony given June 13. To that point it is complete.

On the presence of photographs of Booth, Jefferson Davis, Alexander Stephens and Beauregard at the Surratt house: Anna Surratt testified she had gone one day with Miss Fitzpatrick to a picture gallery to get Miss Fitzpatrick's picture and there they saw Booth's picture on display and each bought one. Anna had hidden her photograph of Booth in the back of a picture called "Morning, Noon and Night," because her brother John had threatened to tear it up when he saw it.[56] The story of the visit to the gallery was corroborated by Miss Fitzpatrick.[57] The photographs of Davis, Stephens, Beauregard, and others were given to Miss Surratt by her father before his death. "I prize them on his account," she said, "if on nobody else's." There were also in the house photographs of Grant, McClellan, and Hooker, she added.[58] This last statement was corroborated by Capt. W. H. Wermerskirch, who was at the Surratt house when the inmates were taken into custody.[59]

In regard to Mrs. Surratt's first trip to Surrattsville on April 11, it was shown that on that occasion she had seen John Nothey concerning some money he owed her. Some years previously Nothey had purchased seventy-five acres of land from John H. Surratt, Sr., and he still owed part of the money. The evidence for this transaction came out in the course of testimony by Weichmann, Nothey, and Captain Gwynn.[60]

[56] Pitman, *The Trial*, 131.

[57] *Ibid.*, 132.

[58] *Ibid.*, 131.

[59] *Ibid.*, 123.

[60] *Ibid.*, 116, Weichmann's testimony, 126, Nothey's testimony, 126, Gwynn's testimony.

It was on this occasion that Booth gave Weichmann ten dollars to hire a buggy with, as Bingham pointed out in his argument. Aiken, in rebuttal, regarded this as proof only of intimacy between Weichmann and the actor. In addition, he could have emphasized that Booth was always free with his money and that it was not strange that Mrs. Surratt, being in need of a buggy, asked this favor of him. And he could have pointed out that when Booth gave Weichmann the ten dollars, the latter accepted it, but now admitted, "I never told Mrs. Surratt that."[61] Thus, whatever the relations between Booth and Weichmann, Mrs. Surratt was never told that Booth had given Weichmann ten dollars to hire the buggy for her first visit to Surrattsville.

On the morning of the fourteenth of April Mrs. Surratt received in her mail this letter from George H. Calvert, Jr.:

Mrs. M. E. Surratt: Riverdale, April 12, 1865

Dear Madam: During a late visit to the lower portion of the county, I ascertained the willingness of Mr. Nothey to settle with you, and desire to call your attention to the fact, in urging the settlement of the claim of my late father's estate. However unpleasant, I must insist upon closing up this matter, and it is imperative, in an early settlement of the estate, which is necessary.

You will, therefore, please inform me at your earliest convenience, as to how and when you will be able to pay the balance remaining due on the land purchased by your late husband.

I am, dear madam, yours respectfully,[62]

[61] *Ibid.*, 117.

[62] *Ibid.*, 126.

It was this letter, according to the defense, which took Mrs. Surratt to Surrattsville on the day of the assassination. She was being pressed for money, and John Nothey owed her $479, plus the interest on it for thirteen years. The letter was entered into the record. John Nothey had gone to Marlboro, probably to avoid her, and, after waiting as late as she could, Mrs. Surratt sent a sharp, brief note to him by Captain Gwynn, Gwynn being a neighbor and her agent in these matters. This note was put into the record.[63] But this entire matter was dismissed as "a pretense" by the Assistant Judge Advocate in his summing up of the evidence, as has been seen.

For just before Mrs. Surratt left Washington on her second trip, John Wilkes Booth dropped by[64] and asked her to take a package to Surrattsville for him. The confusion with regard to what happened to that package can be seen from Bingham's statement. The heart of the matter is whether Mrs. Surratt picked up the package she had given to Mrs. Offutt and handed it to Lloyd. Mrs. Offutt did not know whether she did, but Lloyd swore she had handed him the package. Mrs. Offutt's testimony on June 13 seemed to contradict Lloyd. The examination on this point was as follows:

> Q. Were you standing anywhere at the time Mr. Lloyd came in, so that you could see him when he came in?
> A. Yes sir.
> Q. And did you see Mr. Lloyd while he was standing in the yard?

[63] *Ibid.*, 126.

[64] *Ibid.*, 113, Weichmann's testimony, 131, testimony of Anna Surratt.

A. Yes sir, I did.
Q. Did Mr. Lloyd have in his hands a package while he was standing in the yard?
A. I did not see him have any. . . .
Q. And after Mr. Lloyd came into the house . . . for the first time you saw the package in his hands?
A. Yes sir.
Q. But you did not see it in his hands when he was coming in?
A. No sir, I did not.[65]

It was a small point, but one which directly contradicted a story told by Lloyd.[66] It looks like a choice between the word of Mrs. Offutt and the word of Lloyd.

In that connection it is pertinent to note that Lloyd was drunk that day. This was attested to by all who were on hand and who saw Lloyd, and by Lloyd's own admission.[67] He was so drunk that he could not lie down without being sick. But the court was left with the impression that he was able to tie up Mrs. Surratt's broken buggy, though, according to the bartender, he was "assisting" in fixing it.[68] There the matter rested.

[65] Archives, *Restricted Material,* testimony of June 13.

[66] This testimony does not appear in Pitman's official record.

[67] This admission is not in Pitman's record but can be found in Poore, *Conspiracy Trial,* I, 138–39, and in the *Restricted Material,* testimony by Lloyd, May 15. Others testifying to Lloyd's condition were: Mrs. Offutt; Knott, the bartender; Zad Jenkins, Mrs. Surratt's brother; Captain Gwynn; and also Richard Sweeney and James Lusby, who were at Surrattsville with Lloyd that day. All these statements are adequately given in Pitman's record.

[68] Pitman, *The Trial,* 127. With the word "assisting" Pitman passes over the matter. Knott actually said Lloyd fixed the buggy

Members of the Military Commission
Seated: Col. Clendenin, Brig. Gen. Howe,
Brig. Gen. Ekin, Maj. Gen. Hunter, Brig. Gen. Foster,
Judge Bingham, Judge Holt
Standing: Brig. Gen. Harris, Col. Tompkins,
Maj. Gen. Wallace, Maj. Gen. Kautz, Col. Burnett
Courtesy National Park Service

In regard to Mrs. Surratt's nonrecognition of Payne: Aiken pointed out the fact of her poor eyesight; he failed to point out that Honora Fitzpatrick didn't recognize Payne until his makeshift cap was taken off at police headquarters after his arrest. And Pitman's official record again omits important testimony, for as set forth in the record there is no hint of the fact that one of the arresting police officers claimed the "Gas was turned on full head," and another that "the hall was not lit up very well; we had dimmed the gaslight purposely."[69] But these two men agreed that Mrs. Surratt had said, "Before God, sir, I have not seen that man before." Captain Wermerskirch asserted the dramatic confrontation; Major Smith supported him. Yet Captain Morgan, who was present as the women went out the door, heard nothing, except perhaps Mrs. Surratt mutter something.[70] Honora Fitzpatrick couldn't remember that Mrs. Surratt had said she had not seen this man before.[71] Yet upon this uncertain testimony the Assistant Judge Advocate told of the dramatic incident and said, "The hall was brilliantly lighted."[72]

with some assistance from Weichmann and from Captain Gwynn, he thought. Poore, *Conspiracy Trial,* II, 484–85. Same in *Restricted Material,* May 30 testimony.

[69] Poore, *Conspiracy Trial,* II, 18–19, Smith's testimony; 34–37, Wermerskirch's testimony.

[70] Pitman, *The Trial,* 122.

[71] *Ibid.,* 132.

[72] For what it may be worth, it may be noted that the Washington *Star* for April 22, 1865, gave (with only minor inaccuracies) the details of the arrest of Payne and the Surratt household on April 17, but said not a word of the incident of nonrecognition of Payne by Mrs. Surratt. The government could, of course, have held back this information.

These are the highlights of the testimony in favor of or against Mrs. Surratt. Only one other factor remains to be mentioned: that is the fact to which Reverdy Johnson called attention. "That a woman," said Johnson, "well educated, and, as far as we can judge from all her past life, as we have it in evidence, a devout Christian, ever kind, affectionate and charitable, with no motive disclosed to us that could have caused a total change in her very nature, could have participated in the crimes in question it is almost impossible to believe." There was abundant testimony to Mrs. Surratt's good character.[73] One of the finest tributes came from Louis Weichmann, who said that during all the time he had known her, she was ladylike and exemplary in every particular; her conduct "altogether exemplary." She went to church and "was apparently doing all her duties to God and man up to the time of the assassination."[74]

The commission began its deliberation on June 29 behind closed doors. It debated the fates of the eight prisoners, and, when the verdict and judgment were announced, it found all eight guilty.

[73] Not a witness came forward to attack her character; instead, the prosecution concentrated its fire upon the reputation of her brother, Zad Jenkins. In this connection it may be remarked that a story then current (and often repeated in later years) that slaves once burned the Surratt home because of ill-treatment at the hands of Mrs. Surratt is almost surely a lie. Two Negro witnesses (both former slaves) offered testimony regarding the kind treatment received from Mrs. Surratt. The prosecution brought forth no witnesses to dispute this, nor was any mention ever made at this trial of this story of Mrs. Surratt's cruelty. See Pitman, *The Trial,* 137, 247. For the current story, see the *Star,* July 7, 1865.

[74] Pitman, *The Trial,* 115.

Of the men, Lewis Payne, the cringing Atzerodt, and little Davy Herold were to die by hanging. Dr. Mudd,[75] Arnold, and O'Laughlin were sentenced to life imprisonment at Fort Jefferson, on the Dry Tortugas off the Florida coast. Edward Spangler, sceneshifter at Ford's, charged with aiding Booth's escape, was sentenced to six years at Fort Jefferson.[76]

And what of the woman?

Mrs. Surratt was found guilty of the charge, except for conspiring with Edward Spangler: of this, not guilty. Of the specification, guilty, except as to receiving, sustaining, harboring, and concealing Samuel Arnold and Michael O'Laughlin, and except as to combining and conspiring with Edward Spangler: of this: not guilty.[77]

Under the rules governing the commission, two-thirds of the members had to vote for the death penalty; in the case of Mrs. Surratt this was done only after a plea for clemency had been written to the President, asking him, in consideration of the age and sex of Mrs. Surratt, to commute her sentence to life imprisonment "if he could find it consistent with his sense of duty to the country."[78] We

[75] Mudd was known to have been acquainted with several of the conspirators; that he was acquainted with their machinations was assumed though not conclusively proved. On assassination night he was at his home near Bryantown—nearly thirty miles from Washington—but he had set the leg Booth had broken in his leap from the President's box to the stage of the Ford Theater. Nor had he reported the matter to the authorities until four days later.

[76] O'Laughlin died in prison in 1867. Dr. Mudd, Arnold, and Spangler were pardoned by President Johnson just before he left office, in February, 1869.

[77] Pitman, *The Trial*, 248.

[78] Original in the Archives, *Restricted Material*.

will return later to the long fight over whether the President ever saw this clemency plea; in all events he did not commute the sentence.

Mrs. Surratt was to hang.

CHAPTER III

Mrs. Surratt's Execution: Efforts to Clear Her Name

"The execution of Mrs. Surratt!"
"The execution of Mrs. Surratt!"

THIS excited cry of a newsboy in the street first informed the woman's counsel of the fate of their client. The lawyers were sitting in their offices awaiting the findings of the commission and were considerably startled by the announcement, as many of the older bar members were predicting Mrs. Surratt's acquittal.[1] "So sudden was the shock, so unexpected the result, amazed beyond expression at the celerity of the order of execution, we hardly knew how to proceed," wrote John Clampitt. But they had to proceed with all haste if the woman was to be saved, for it was now five o'clock on Thursday afternoon, July 6, and the Presidential order of the previous

[1] Clampitt, *loc. cit.*, 234. The Washington *Star* reported that the sentence was "rather more sudden than was expected, and occasioned some surprise, though everyone approved." Washington *Evening Star*, July 7, 1865.

day (just now made public) set the execution to take place on July 7, between the hours of ten and two.[2]

The counsel tried to reach the President but were turned back. They wired Reverdy Johnson in Baltimore, who told them to get a writ of habeas corpus, though it was nearly midnight on the sixth. They called on Judge Wylie at two o'clock in the morning, and he issued the writ, though in doing so he observed that his act might land him in the Old Capitol before the day was out. Clampitt gave the writ to the United States marshal at four o'clock on the morning of July 7, to be served on General Hancock. At ten o'clock President Johnson, in the Executive Office, wrote a note to the General, which read:

> I, Andrew Johnson, President of the United States, do hereby declare that the writ of Habeas Corpus has been heretofore suspended in such cases as this, and I do hereby especially suspend this writ, and direct that you proceed to execute the order heretofore given upon the judgment of the Military Commission and you will give this order in return to this writ.[3]

At ten minutes past twelve o'clock noon General Hancock, accompanied by the Attorney General, appeared before Judge Wylie with the order suspending the writ, and Clampitt felt that "all hope faded for Mrs. Surratt."[4]

After the announcement of the findings there was "a rush" to the White House, according to the *Star,* but friends

[2] Pitman, *The Trial,* 249.

[3] Original in the Archives, Records of the District Court, District of Columbia, Habeas Corpus No. 46. But this, and the application for the writ are in Pitman, *The Trial,* 250.

[4] Clampitt, *loc. cit.,* 238.

of the condemned were referred by the President to the Judge Advocate General, who remained unmoved. "Mrs. Surratt's case was the most strongly urged," the *Star* reported.

Anna Surratt went to the White House the evening of the announcement and again on the morning of the seventh, when she saw the President's military secretary, General Mussey, who told her Johnson's orders "were imperative, and he would receive no one." Miss Surratt sat in the East Room for several hours in the hope of seeing the President.[5] Only one person reached Johnson's ear that day: the widow of Stephen A. Douglas pushed aside the bayonets and pleaded for Mrs. Surratt's life, but the President was adamant, and she could do nothing.

Meanwhile, back at the penitentiary, those to be hanged learned of the findings. The sentences were read to them about noon on the day before they were to die. Even the stolid Payne's fortitude was shaken by the hurried way in which he was to be executed,[6] and Mrs. Surratt "burst into a violent paroxysm of grief" and asked for Fathers Walter and Wiget, her daughter Anna, and John P. Brophy, a friend of Weichmann's who had interested himself in her case.[7] Payne sent for Captain Rath and told him, "Captain, if I had two lives to give, I'd give one gladly to save Mrs. Surratt. I know that she is innocent, and would never die in this way if I hadn't been found at her house. She knew nothing about the conspiracy at all, and is an innocent woman." Captain Rath conferred with Major Eckert,

[5] Washington *Evening Star*, July 7, 1865.

[6] Doster, *op. cit.*, 271.

[7] Washington *Evening Star*, July 7, 1865.

Payne's statement was taken, and Rath felt the woman would be saved after all.[8] On the same day Payne told Father Walter that he believed and was convinced that she was innocent.[9] And on the day of the execution Payne told General Hartranft that "he was convinced that Mrs. Surratt was innocent of the murder of the President or any knowledge thereof—and as to the abduction of the President he did not know that she was connected with it, although he had frequent conversations with her, during his stay at her house." The General added, "I think Payne would state the truth in this matter."[10] It is not known whether or not any of these appeals ever reached the President.

Captain Rath instructed the prison carpenter to construct a gallows and tested it himself with a bag of shot.[11] The workmen around the prison were superstitious, and he had to ask soldiers to dig the graves. For coffins, he got boxes from the navy yard. By eleven o'clock on Friday morning the gallows were ready.[12]

The drop was tested at twenty-five minutes after eleven. It was a hot, windless, suffocating day, and the crowd grew impatient when the prisoners still had not appeared by one o'clock, and rumors spread that a reprieve was the cause

[8] Gray, *loc. cit.*, 635.

[9] Rev. Jacob A. Walter, letter to the President, Archives, RG 153, JAO, Box 3, unnumbered item. Letter dated July 7, 1865.

[10] General J. F. Hartranft, Archives, RG 153, JAO, Box 3, unnumbered item. This statement by the General is on the second sheet of the folded paper on which appears Father Walter's quotation of Payne.

[11] Gray, *loc. cit.*, 635.

[12] Washington *Evening Star*, July 7, 1865.

of the delay. Many believed Mrs. Surratt would not hang —among them the hangman himself. He later recalled that he only put five knots in her rope, "for I fully expected that Mrs. Surratt would never hang."[13] But at fifteen minutes after one the procession began. The prisoners walked the short distance to the gallows, up the fifteen creaking, railed steps, and were seated before the dangling ropes. Then General Hartranft read the death warrant to them. Finally General Hancock appeared and ordered the executioner to proceed. "Her, too?" Rath asked, and was told that she could not be saved. Then General Hancock stationed himself at the east end of the building, still awaiting a reprieve should one come.[14] But at twenty-six minutes after one the drops fell from under the scaffold. At sixteen minutes until two the prison doctor pronounced the four dead; ten minutes later they were cut down, placed in boxes, and buried a few feet south of the scaffold near the prison wall.[15]

[13] Gray, *loc. cit.*, 635.

[14] Clampitt, *loc. cit.*, 238.

[15] The Washington *Star* reported that friends of Mrs. Surratt, Herold, and Atzerodt tried to get the bodies, but that the authorities declined "for the present." The New York *Tribune* of July 17 added many details. According to the *Tribune*, friends of Mrs. Surratt had an undertaker waiting, and Stanton, when petitioned, referred them to Judge Advocate Holt; Holt referred them to Stanton; Stanton sent them back to Holt; Holt sent them back to Stanton; Stanton back to Holt—who at last sent a verbal message through a clerk to deny the request. Anna Surratt requested her mother's body from President Johnson, February 5, 1869, and the request was granted. See Andrew Johnson Papers, Library of Congress, Manuscript Division, Ac. 6261 (photostatic copy of request).

On the day of the execution hundreds of people, old and young, male and female, visited the vicinity of the Surratt house, and the misery of Anna Surratt was "the talk of the city."[16] Still, the newspapers unhesitatingly described Mrs. Surratt as "one of the most active and energetic of the conspirators,"[17] to use the words of the Washington *Daily Chronicle*, and agreed that there was no doubt that she had aided them in every way.

But hardly was the woman executed before new information about her began to appear in the newspapers. On July 11 the Washington *Constitutional Union* published a sensational affidavit by John P. Brophy—the affidavit which the Washington *National Intelligencer* had turned down earlier because it was "too strong."[18] This affidavit Brophy had written out and sworn to on the day of the execution, but he never received a reply when it was sent to the War Department, and President Johnson thought it "wholly without weight" and so refused to interfere in the hanging.[19]

This Brophy statement is interesting and is reprinted in full here for the first time. It reads:

1. I can have it proved, if time be allowed, that Weichmann "is and always was a *coward*" according to his father's words.

2. That since this trial closed, he told me that he was arrested as a conspirator and threatened with death by Mr. Stan-

[16] G. A. Townsend, *Life, Crime and Capture of John Wilkes Booth*, 78.

[17] Washington *Daily Morning Chronicle*, July 8, 1865.

[18] Brophy in the *Washington Post*, January 7, 1908.

[19] Brophy in the *Washington Post*, July 21, 1901.

ton and Mr. Burnett unless he would at once reveal all about the assassination—they [Mr. Stanton and Mr. Burnett] alleging that he [Weichmann] knew all about it.

3. That since this trial closed he told me he would rather be hooted at as a spy and informer, and do anything rather than be tried as a conspirator, and have his future hopes blasted.

4. That since this trial closed, he told me if Captain Gleason had not informed on him, they [Stanton and Burnett and the rest] "never would have got a word" out of him about any of the parties suspected.

5. That since this trial closed, he has admitted to me he was a liar.

6. That he swore to a deliberate falsehood on the witness stand.

7. That a short time before the assassination, he introduced Atzerodt to me as a particular friend, and that the same day he and Atzerodt were riding on Booth's horses.

8. That about the same time, he boasted in the office where he worked that he could make forty thousand dollars any day he liked, but that it would be made dishonorably. This he told me himself since the close of the trial. I can bring other and new witnesses to prove his intimacy with Atzerodt.

9. That he told me since the trial closed, that Mrs. Surratt wept bitterly and constantly at the thought of John [her son] going to Richmond, and that she begged and implored him not to go to Richmond, but to stop at home, and not bring trouble upon himself and upon the family.

10. That he [Weichmann] told me since the close of the trial that once while some of these men were in the house with John [her son] Mrs. Surratt called John [her son] aside and said to him, "John! there is something going on I am afraid, and I cannot see what it must be. Why do these

men come here? Now, John, I cannot allow this, and you must tell me what you are about." Weichmann also told me John did not and would not tell her why the men were there, or what they were about.

11. That since the trial closed, he told me he thought Mrs. Surratt to be innocent, saying her son John was the guilty one; and he offered to give me a letter to President Johnson in her favor, *providing I should keep it a profound secret* and hand the letter to the President myself.

I asked him why he did not write a similar letter to Judge Holt, and he said he would not—that he "had no confidence in Holt."

12. That he was an avowed Secessionist, and told me he wished to go to Richmond to get a clerkship, saying he would not work under this government if he could get anything else to do.

13. That he went away to shun the draft, and told me so himself, saying he would never fight for the Northern side, and saying also, that if drafted he would "pocket his share of the 'club money' and clear out."

14. That he had me summoned to testify to his character and afterwards, remembering I suppose all that he had said to me, begged me and brought some of the sub-officers of the court to get me to leave the witness room for fear I would be called upon the stand.

15. That he told me since the trial closed that twenty-five thousand dollars were offered to the detective who had him in charge to bring him back from Canada.

16. Many other important facts in Mrs. Surratt's favor can be brought to light if time be allowed for that purpose.

John P. Brophy.[20]

[20] John P. Brophy, statement, Archives, RG 153, JAO, Box 3, unnumbered item.

Weichmann's answer to this affidavit was to deny it, and for the first time he asserted, "I do not believe she is innocent." But he added, "I partly made a promise to her friends which on account of circumstances I do not deem it prudent to fulfill." And he also made an admission: "Mrs. Surratt some time in Feby did remark that Booth and John appeared to have business together and that he [*sic*] was bound to find it out. She went into the parlor and spoke to John but whether she found out their business I do not know."[21] Here Weichmann admitted that as of sometime in February, at least so far as he knew, Mrs. Surratt did not know what business Booth had with her son. Also he made it clear that he did not know if she ever found out what that business was. This admission, had it been made at the trial, would not have harmed Mrs. Surratt's case.

While the public was thinking over Brophy's charges, the New York *Times* opined (on July 13) that the friends of Mrs. Surratt were mistaken in trying to keep her name before the public. Let the matter rest was the *Times'* advice.

But on the day after Brophy's affidavit was published in Washington, the New York *Tribune* printed a dispatch from Washington which kept Mrs. Surratt's name very much before the public. This dispatch quoted one of the woman's counsel as saying "positively" that spiritual advisers were denied her until they had promised not to proclaim belief in her innocence. Then, on July 17, the *Tribune* published the following story:

On July 6, Father Walter had asked for a pass from the War Department to enable him to visit Mrs. Surratt,

[21] Weichmann to Colonel Burnett, Archives, RG 153, JAO, Box 3, "W," 32.

and when a messenger brought him the pass, Walter expressed the belief that Mrs. Surratt was innocent. An hour later General Hardie called on him and told him the pass he had received was not good unless signed by Stanton, and then Hardie asked Father Walter to promise to say nothing of Mrs. Surratt's innocence, "and I will give you the necessary pass." Walter told Hardie he would continue to express his belief, when Hardie observed that "as yet" there were no charges against him (Father Walter) in the War Department. Then Walter told Hardie he would proclaim the woman's innocence, and the War Department could hang him, too, "if it thought proper." But as Hardie was about to go, Walter agreed to the condition in order that Mrs. Surratt might not die unabsolved.[22]

In this story, too, the *Tribune* pointed out that Brophy could not be used by Mrs. Surratt's counsel "because they were not allowed to recall Weichmann to lay the foundation for his impeachment by Brophy." This story is corroborated by Mrs. Surratt's counsel.[23]

On July 21, General Hardie, in a letter to the agent of the Associated Press, undertood to answer the *Tribune* story of his denial of a pass to Father Walter. General Hardie confirmed that he granted the pass. He related how his agent came back from Father Walter and informed him "of the violent and excited language" Father Walter had used. Hardie said he then went to caution Father Walter as "a well-wisher and as a friend of the church" to say nothing because of the "great public excitement." Hardie in-

[22] New York *Tribune,* July 17, 1865.

[23] Clampitt, *loc. cit., 234.* Clampitt related what efforts were made to get Brophy on the witness stand.

sisted he went quite on his own, with his motive to "restrain imprudent and mischievous discussions." The visit was not known to or suggested by Stanton. Hardie said he did not extract a promise from Father Walter to say nothing of Mrs. Surratt's innocence. "Annoyed by what he had said, I was about, however, to leave the room and to defer giving him the pass . . . when he said, 'I promise.' " And lastly, Hardie repeated that Stanton "made no condition."[24]

From this exchange the reader may make up his own mind whether or not a promise was extracted from Father Walter. It is still not clear whether Stanton sent General Hardie to Father Walter. It is clear that General Hancock went to Walter's superior, Bishop Spaulding, in Baltimore, and asked him to enjoin silence on Father Walter. Father Walter revealed years later that Spaulding wrote to him asking him to say nothing, and Father Walter asserted that the Bishop told Hancock "he also believed her an innocent woman." Bishop Spaulding wrote General Hardie expressing his regret at Hardie's action and assuring him that Father Walter had been "cautioned" to "observe silence," and that he had promised to do so.[25] General Hancock was sent to call on the Bishop; it may be a coincidence that another general called on Father Walter. We have Hardie's word he was not sent on this mission. There is no proof.

John Coyle, one of the editors of the Washington *National Intelligencer*, talked to Father Walter on the day

[24] Brevet Brigadier General James A. Hardie, in the New York *Tribune*, July 21, 1865.

[25] Letter from Bishop Spaulding to General Hardie, Hardie Papers, Manuscript Division, Library of Congress, 1844–86, AC. 1704.

Mrs. Surratt was condemned. Father Walter told him of the incident—of how an officer (whose name Coyle withheld) told him he must be quiet or he would be denied the right to administer last rites to Mrs. Surratt. Said Coyle, "Those who remember Father Walter will readily conceive how he would receive such a message." Father Walter told the officer he would proclaim her innocence while he lived, and the officer could tell his superiors that. Father Walter also told Coyle that he had received orders from Bishop Spaulding forbidding him to make further statements, and that General Hancock had visited Spaulding, under orders of the War Department, to elicit the statement.[26]

That was all the public knew of the affair and of Father Walter until John Clampitt wrote his article on Mrs. Surratt fifteen years later. Then Clampitt told of another incident between Mrs. Surratt and Father Walter. He quotes Mrs. Surratt as saying to Father Walter, "Holy Father, can I not tell these people before I die that I am innocent of the crime for which I have been condemned to death?" and Clampitt said Father Walter replied, "No, my child, the world and all that is in it has now receded forever. It would do no good, and it might disturb the serenity of your last moments!" This incident, Clampitt thought, "should for ever set at rest the question of the guilt or innocence of this poor woman."[27]

Finally, after a silence of twenty-five years, Father Walter spoke out. He denied Clampitt's story of his having prohibited Mrs. Surratt from asserting her innocence; he

[26] John Coyle, "Was Mrs. Surratt Guilty," date and paper unknown.

[27] Clampitt, *loc. cit.*, 239.

East End of the Old Penitentiary as it is today.
The Surratt trial was held on the third floor
of this section of the prison

Courtesy National Park Service

told a simpler, less dramatic story. He said, "Shortly before the hour of her execution, Mrs. Surratt was brought out of her cell and was sitting on a chair at the doorway. It was at this time that she made clearly and distinctly the solemn declaration of her innocence. 'Father, I wish to say something.' 'Well what is it my child?' 'That I am innocent.' " Those, according to Father Walter, were Mrs. Surratt's "exact words ... the last confession of an innocent woman."[28]

Father Walter explained that he had waited a quarter of a century to permit people to calm down, to lay aside prejudices. Speaking at a meeting of the Catholic Historical Society in New York about the same time, he said of Mrs. Surratt: "I attended to her spiritual wants until she went to the scaffold. I cannot of course violate my vows to the church and tell the secrets of the confessional, but I will say that from what I know, Mrs. Surratt was innocent of any complicity in that great crime." And he added that he believed she died "as innocent of that crime as a babe unborn."[29]

Whether Mrs. Surratt declared her innocence to Father Walter, an echo of such a declaration reached the public when the New York *Times* reported she said, when told of her sentence to death, "I had no hand in the murder of the President."[30]

[28] Reverend J. A. Walter, *Church News*, August 16, 1891, paper read before U. S. Catholic Historical Society, May 25, 1891.

[29] "Mrs. Surratt's Case," undated clipping, unidentified newspaper. In the Washingtoniana collection, Vol. 3 of clippings dealing with Lincoln's death, Washington Public Library, Washington, D. C.

[30] New York *Times*, July 8, 1865.

Of his controversy with Hardie, Father Walter said that he remarked to an orderly who delivered his first pass that he had read all the evidence, "and, as regards Mrs. Surratt, there was not enough evidence to hang a cat." He related how Hardie asked him to promise to say nothing, and he gave his final answer to Hardie, "I cannot let Mrs. Surratt die without the sacraments, so if I must say yes, I say yes."[31] This is substantially the same story the New York *Tribune* carried on July 17, 1865.

From all this it can be seen that at least two voices proclaimed the innocence of Mrs. Surratt. On the day of her execution she had asked John Brophy to try, "at some future time, when the passions of the war are cooled, the task of clearing her name of the crime. . . ." This he had promised to do, and he worked to that end until his death. Father Walter was hardly less diligent.

Then, in the spring of 1867, a new defender joined the lists. The country was treated to the unlikely spectacle of Benjamin F. Butler, of Massachusetts, defending a Southern lady! How the man whose famous Order Number 28 won for him the nickname "Beast Butler" in the South came to rise to Mrs. Surratt's defense is interesting.[32] It came about this way:

In the course of a debate over the relief of the destitute in the South, Congressman John A. Bingham (the same

[31] Rev. Walter, *Church News*, August 16, 1891.

[32] For a Southern woman on Butler, see Mary Boykin Chesnut, *A Diary from Dixie*, 164–65. Order Number 28 decreed that New Orleans women who insulted Union soldiers would be treated as women of the town. New Orleans was, of course, under Butler's control at that time.

Bingham who had been special judge advocate at the trial of the conspirators) twitted Butler on his failure to take Fort Fisher, calling him "the hero of Fort Fisher *not* taken."[33] To this Butler replied that he had done all he could against the enemies of his country—"the best I could," he said. And he went on:

> The only victim of that gentleman's prowess that I know of was an innocent woman hung upon the scaffold, one Mrs. Surratt. And I can sustain the memory of Fort Fisher if he and his present associates can sustain him in shedding the blood of a woman tried by a military commission and convicted without sufficient evidence in my judgment.[34]

To this Bingham replied that he stood on his record, and he asked, "What does the gentleman know of the evidence in the case, and what does he care?"[35]

Five days later Butler took fifteen minutes to answer Bingham. He began by asserting that Bingham erred in saying he was "the advocate of the United States only." He pointed out:

> Sir, he makes a wide mistake as to his official position. He was the special judge advocate whose duty it was to protect the rights of the prisoners as well as the rights of the United States, and to sum up the evidence and state the law as would a judge on the bench. Certainly it was his duty to present to the commission all the evidence bearing upon the case.

[33] This reference is to Butler's unsuccessful attempt to take Fort Fisher, North Carolina, late in 1864.

[34] *Congressional Globe*, 40 Cong., 1 sess. (March 21, 1867), 263.

[35] Ibid., 263–64.

Then, said Butler, Bingham had within his possession and knowledge a piece of evidence he did not present: Booth's diary. "That diary," he said, "came into the possession of the Government, but it was not brought before the military commission. Although even Booth's tobacco pipe, spur, and compass, found in the same pocket with the diary, were put in evidence." And eighteen pages are now missing from this diary, "although the edges as yet show they had all been written over." Butler asked, "Was the diary whole when it came into the hands of the Government? . . . If it was good judgment on the part of the gentleman prosecuting the assassins of the President to put in evidence the tobacco pipe, which was found in Booth's pocket, why was not the diary, in his own handwriting, put in evidence, and wherein he himself had detailed the particulars of that crime?" Butler asked again and again, "Who spoliated that book? Who suppressed that evidence?"

Butler dwelt on a passage still in the spoliated book: Booth's remark, "I propose to return to Washington and give myself up, and clear myself from this great crime."[36] "How clear himself?" Butler asked. "By disclosing his accomplices? Who were they?"

"I understand," said Butler, "the theory to be that that evidence was not produced lest Booth's glorification of himself, as found in his diary, should go before the country. I think that a lame excuse. If an assassin can glorify himself, let him do so. No harm could result from it." But-

[36] Butler quoted this passage from memory. It reads, "I have . . . almost a mind to return to Washington and in a measure clear my name, which I feel I can do." Booth, Diary, in the Lincoln Museum, Washington, D. C.

ler then spells out what the suppression of the diary shows, in his judgment: "that up to a certain hour Booth contemplated capture and abduction, and that he afterward changed his purpose to assassination."

He pointed out that Mrs. Surratt may or may not have known of the change of purpose. "And if Mrs. Surratt did not know of this change of purpose there is no evidence that she knew in any way of the assassination and ought not, in my judgment, to have been convicted of taking part in it."

Butler especially indicted Bingham: "Now, what I find fault with in the judge advocate, who did not sum up for the prisoner, is that in his very able and very bitter argument against the prisoners no notice is taken . . . of this change of purpose and brought to the attention of . . . that military tribunal." Butler closed with the point that if we had all the evidence, "we might then be able to find who, indeed, changed Booth's purpose . . . who it was that could profit by assassination who could not profit by capture and abduction . . . who it was expected by Booth would succeed to Lincoln if the knife made a vacancy."[37]

When Bingham replied to Butler's attack, he could not answer the question, "Who spoliated the book?" "That," he said, "is about as interesting a cry as 'Who Killed Cock Robin?' " Bingham denied that he spoliated the diary and correctly pointed out that it was the Judge Advocate General—not he—who was the "official recorder" at the conspiracy trial, though Bingham went on to defend the Judge Advocate as "above reproach." As to the change of plan on Booth's part, Bingham said it "was exhibited in evidence

[37] *Congressional Globe*, 40 Cong., 1 sess. (March 26, 1867), 363.

on the trial that the original plan, as falsely alleged by the conspirators, was to kidnap, not to assassinate."[38]

It was unfortunate that Butler's whole interest in the cause of Mrs. Surratt was confined to using it as a tool with which to belabor President Johnson—as his closing remark clearly shows. He was infinitely more interested in finding evidence that Johnson was a co-conspirator than in showing that Mrs. Surratt was not. In taking up the case, he was most successful in compounding the confusion.

In the course of his remarks Butler alleged that the government had deliberately suppressed Booth's diary, but the actual reasons for its failure to appear in the evidence were not and are not now known. He asked who mutilated Booth's diary, but he asked in vain; John Bingham only replied that *he* had not mutilated the diary, and Butler's question remains unanswered today.

But Butler did a real service for Mrs. Surratt when he pointed out that even if Mrs. Surratt knew of the first plot against the President, there is nothing in the record to show that she necessarily knew of the plot to assassinate Lincoln. If she did know of the kidnap scheme but was not appraised of the changed objective, then Butler's argument is valid, and she ought not to have been hanged as party to the assassination plot.

Mrs. Surratt's cause was a means to an end for Benjamin Butler. For John Brophy and Father Walter her cause was more in the nature of a crusade to clear her name. Others who espoused the cause for still different reasons were yet to be heard from.

[38] *Ibid.*, 364.

CHAPTER IV

The Second Trial of Mrs. Surratt

MRS. Surratt was tried all over again at the trial of her son in 1867. All of the evidence against her was aired, this time in open court. A flood of light was cast upon the character and motives of her two principal accusers, John M. Lloyd and Louis J. Weichmann, and upon various other matters. Because it was her son who was on trial, no adequate review has ever been made of the points at issue involving the mother.

When John H. Surratt was brought back to Washington to face trial two years after his mother's death,[1] he was

[1] While the conspiracy trial was in progress in May and June, 1865, John Surratt was sheltered by a Catholic priest near Montreal. In September he sailed to Liverpool, where he was detected but not arrested. From Liverpool he made his way to Rome and joined the Papal Zouaves. Recognized and informed against by an old friend of his and Weichmann's, Surratt was arrested but escaped by leaping into an abyss and landing on a ledge of rock. He then left Papal territory, reached Naples, and sailed to Alexandria, Egypt, where, on November 26, 1866, he was at last taken prisoner by the United States Consul General. In mid-December he was sent home in irons aboard the United States vessel *Swatara*.

assured of a trial by jury in a criminal court. Thanks to the famous Milligan decision of the previous year, military commissions authorized by the President, such as the one that had tried the conspirators, were declared unlawful. In a decision that sounded strangely like an echo of Reverdy Johnson's argument, the Supreme Court held that martial rule "can never exist where the courts are open," and the only disagreement among the judges was whether Congress (not the President) had power to make provision for military trial.[2]

A number of reviews of the case made out against John H. Surratt are available;[3] another review is not necessary. The trial opened June 10, 1867, in the criminal court for the District of Columbia, Judge Fisher presiding, and it

---

There seemed a curious reluctance on the part of the American government at this time to ever capture Surratt. A House of Representatives Judiciary Committee investigated and discovered that no demand for Surratt was ever made on the English government after he was known to be in Liverpool. In fact, the State Department informed the consulate in Liverpool that, after consultation with the Secretary of War and the Judge Advocate General, it was thought "advisable that no action be taken" in regard to Surratt's arrest. Surely, for whatever reasons, no eagerness was shown by the governmental authorities to prosecute young Surratt. See 39 Cong., 2 sess., *House Executive Document No. 9*, and *Report No. 33*.

[2] *Ex Parte Milligan*, 4 Wallace 2 (1866). See also Charles Warren, *The Supreme Court in United States History*, III, 145 ff.

[3] For a review of the trial favorable to young Surratt, see Eisenschiml, *In the Shadow*, "The Surratt Trial," 265–348. For a review adverse to him, see T. M. Harris, *Assassination of Lincoln*, 260 ff.

closed sixty-two days later. It was not conclusively shown that Surratt was in Washington on the night of the assassination; the jury could not agree, the case was *nol-prossed,* and Surratt went free.

In the course of the trial the case of Mrs. Surratt was heard in detail, the old witnesses returning to testify and some new witnesses appearing for the first time. Out of the mass of contradictory statements, some interesting facts became apparent.

John M. Lloyd was a reluctant witness at the trial of young Surratt. When asked if he was a witness at the conspiracy trial, he replied, "Yes, sir, unfortunately."[4] Asked to repeat Mrs. Surratt's conversation with him on Tuesday (at his first meeting with her, on the road at Uniontown), Lloyd said, "I do not wish to state one single solitary word more than I am compelled to." When told by the prosecution that that made no difference and asked to state what Mrs. Surratt said, Lloyd said, "I cannot do it unless I do it my own way. It is out of the question." When told to give the substance, he said she told him to have the guns ready, that they would be wanted, called for, or something—"I forgot which." He said either expression satisfied him. The prosecution told him it did not matter what he was satisfied about. Lloyd said he wanted to state his reasons, but the prosecution told him, "We do not care about your reasons." Then Lloyd repeated that he told Mrs. Surratt he was afraid the house would be searched and that he was thinking of having the guns buried, or something.

Of his conversation with Mrs. Surratt on the road to

[4] *Surratt Trial,* I, 276.

Uniontown, Lloyd said it was "in an ordinary tone of voice," and "there was nothing like a whisper."[5]

Of his conversation with Mrs. Surratt on the day of the assassination, Lloyd said he didn't get home until late and had been drinking, so he did not recall just when he got home: "I do not remember distinctly, but it appears to me, in the confused memory I have of it, that the sun was not more than half an hour high. . . . I was in liquor at the time, and being so, I did not want to have any conversation with her." He said he was sick from liquor, but fixed Mrs. Surratt's buggy spring with some yarn. He said she gave him a package which he later found to contain a field glass, but he did not know whether he would recognize the glass, now. When shown the glass, he said, "It is my impression that this is not the kind of a one I saw." He thought it was similar, but not the glass Mrs. Surratt gave him and which he in turn gave to Booth.[6] Lloyd further admitted that he was so intoxicated that day he "never could remember even who took my horse and buggy." He explained liquor had a peculiar effect on him: "A very singular effect, upon my mind, chiefly. It makes me forget a great many things."[7] Asked by the defense, "I understand you to say . . . that whisky has a remarkable effect upon your mind, in blurring your recollection?" Lloyd replied, "So it does; it always did."[8] Lloyd flatly admitted he was drunk and said, "I cannot in justice to myself taste any liquor, without making me possibly say something, or use some expression, that I

[5] *Ibid.*, I, 295, 299.
[6] *Ibid.*, I, 288.
[7] *Ibid.*, I, 293.
[8] *Ibid.*, I, 296.

would not wish to, or oftentimes making me forget things I do not wish to forget."[9]

But more important than all the doubt he cast on his previous testimony was Lloyd's admission (if he is to be believed) that he was testifying at the conspiracy trial under threats and promises. A detective named Cottingham had testified at that trial that he had obtained Lloyd's confession "through strategy."[10] Two years later Lloyd probably revealed what Cottingham meant. Asked if Cottingham had made any promises of reward for his confession, Lloyd said, "I can only state that Mr. Cottingham . . . stated . . . that the government would protect me and my property and support me, and see that I was returned home." In addition, he said that, when he was in prison, an officer of the government told him he wanted a statement.

> I told him I had made a fuller statement to Col. Wells than I could possibly do to him under the circumstances, while things were fresh in my memory. His reply was that it was not full enough. . . . When I told him what I had repeated before, that I did not remember any person saying thus and so, he jumps up very quick off his seat, as if very mad, and asked me if I knew what I was guilty of. I told him, under the circumstances, I did not. He said you are guilty as an accessory to a crime, the punishment of which is death.[11]

The other chief witness against Mrs. Surratt, Louis Weichmann, also encountered some difficulties while on

[9] *Ibid.*, I, 298.

[10] Pitman, *The Trial*, 125.

[11] *Surratt Trial*, I, 290.

the witness stand. Certain of his stories were contradicted, others shown to be discrepant.

So involved and confusing is this mass of testimony and countertestimony, it will perhaps be best to take each item in Weichmann's charges against Mrs. Surratt and to follow it with the defense statement. Proceeding along this line, then:

(1) Weichmann said that one evening in March he, Anna Surratt, her mother, and Misses Jenkins and Fitzpatrick were returning from church, when Mrs. Surratt went into the Herndon House, saying "she was going in to see Payne."[12]

This visit to the Herndon House was admitted by the young ladies—but they denied Mrs. Surratt said she was going to see Payne, or that she ever explained why she went in at all.[13] Why she went into the hotel was never cleared up; but Weichmann's assertion as to what she said was contradicted by the other members of the party.

(2) On Mrs. Surratt's trip to Surrattsville the day she met Lloyd, Weichmann said Mrs. Surratt talked to Lloyd in a confidential way, in a low tone of voice. Cross-examined he said his conspiracy-trial testimony, that Mrs. Surratt whispered to Lloyd, and his present testimony, that she used a low tone, were the same.[14]

But Weichmann admitted that, while he was driving to prison with Lloyd in the course of the conspiracy trial, Lloyd "expressed astonishment" when told that Weich-

[12] *Ibid.*, I, 385.

[13] *Ibid.*, I, 235, 715, testimony of Honora Fitzpatrick; also II, 747, testimony of Olivia Jenkins.

[14] *Ibid.*, I, 446.

mann had testified that Lloyd's conversation with Mrs. Surratt was whispered.[15]

Lloyd had testified that this conversation was in an ordinary tone; Weichmann, that it was whispered. It was no doubt in an effort to bring these two contradictory statements more into harmony that Weichmann testified at the Surratt trial that "a low tone" of voice was used, and that he meant the expression to be the equivalent of "a whisper." The contradiction suggests Weichmann did, in fact, hear the conversation.[16]

(3) On Mrs. Surratt's trip to Surrattsville on the day of the assassination, Weichmann said Booth came into the house as he went to get the buggy for her trip. He testified that, as they were leaving, Mrs. Surratt said she must go back to get "those things" of Booth's, and that she told him "it was glass." Weichmann asserted that there were some pickets on the grass, three miles out of town, and that Mrs. Surratt "asked these soldiers" how long they would be on duty; when they told her they would be withdrawn at eight o'clock, she said: "I'm glad to know it."[17] According to Weichmann, Mrs. Surratt was "lively and cheerful" on the way down to Surrattsville.[18] Weichmann also declared that Lloyd fixed Mrs. Surratt's buggy for her.

[15] *Ibid.*, I, 416.

[16] When Weichmann was first committed to Carroll Prison, he admitted that he had heard this conversation between Lloyd and Mrs. Surratt and disclosed that it was in relation to the blockade-runner, Howell. See Weichmann's statement to Colonel Wood, Archives, RG 153, JAO, Box 3.

[17] *Surratt Trial*, I, 391.

[18] *Ibid.*, 391.

The defense remarked that, at the conspiracy trial, Weichmann had said that after seeing Booth come in, he had gone upstairs, and when he came down he saw Booth and Mrs. Surratt standing in the same places he had just now described as finding them after getting back with the buggy. Weichmann said his memory was more distinct after two years—he explained he was "nervous" at the conspiracy trial. Weichmann claimed it only took him seven or eight minutes to get the buggy and return; though under examination he admitted he went to the post office and mailed a letter while out to get the buggy. In fact, he claimed that he walked to Howard's stable, ordered a buggy, walked to the post office, left a letter, got the buggy, and went back to Mrs. Surratt's—all in ten minutes.[19] When reminded that at the previous trial he had said Mrs. Surratt and Booth could not have been together over three or four minutes, Weichman did not remember he had said that.[20]

As to the story of the pickets, not a word of it was heard at the previous trial. It was first incorporated in a letter given by Weichmann to Pitman in August, 1865—as were other hitherto unheard of points against Mrs. Surratt which Weichmann "recalled" after her execution. In the Pitman record, Weichmann said Mrs. Surratt asked "an old farmer" about the pickets and was informed they would be withdrawn at eight o'clock, whereupon she said she "was glad to know it."[21] The defense missed a point by not asking Weichmann if Mrs. Surratt asked "an old farmer," or, as

[19] *Ibid.*, 444.

[20] *Ibid.*, 445.

[21] Pitman, *The Trial*, 420, Weichmann's post-trial statement, dated August 11, 1865.

he stated in the Surratt trial, "these soldiers" themselves. Further, it was remarked by one of the defense witnesses that, although he came to town nearly every day at this period, he never saw pickets beyond the District line.[22] The government never tried to establish that pickets were at the point in question.

As to the belabored point of who fixed Mrs. Surratt's broken buggy, Lloyd claimed that he had mended it, and was supported by Weichmann. At the conspiracy trial John Knott, the bartender, had cast some doubt on this by saying he saw Captain Gwynn and Weichmann and Lloyd all at the buggy at the same time. The Judge Advocate had asked quickly if Knott didn't recall that Gwynn had gone before Lloyd arrived, and Knott replied that he recalled nothing of the sort.[23] Gwynn, on the witness stand again, told the whole story. He said he arrived at Surrattsville before Lloyd, and as he was helping Mrs. Surratt into her buggy, he noticed it was broken and called her attention to the fact that it was not safe. Then he asked Knott to get a piece of rope and explained to Weichmann how to fix it; his wife being sick, Gwynn left before Lloyd arrived.[24] Why Gwynn had not made this clear earlier is a mystery. Much was made of the fact that Lloyd was sober enough to fix a buggy.

(4) Weichmann testified that at supper on the evening of the assassination someone came to the door; that Mrs. Surratt went upstairs and answered it, and that he heard footsteps in the parlor. Also, he said that later, in the par-

[22] *Surratt Trial,* II, 758, testimony of B. F. Gwynn.

[23] Poore, *Conspiracy Trial,* II, 485.

[24] *Surratt Trial,* II, 756, testimony of B. F. Gwynn.

lor, Mrs. Surratt was nervous and asked him to pray for her intentions.[25]

Weichmann had mentioned this mysterious visitor at the trial of the conspirators,[26] but he was not identified, and nothing more was said of him. In his post-trial statement to Pitman, Weichmann for the first time boldly said the visitor was Booth. In this statement, too, he revealed for the first time that Mrs. Surratt was nervous, agitated, and restless that evening.[27]

The defense produced testimony to show (a) that it was Anna, not her mother, who answered the door;[28] (b) that it was a naval captain named Scott who called, and that he came to leave some papers for Miss Jenkins;[29] (c) that no one else in the parlor noticed Mrs. Surratt's being nervous, and no one heard her ask Weichmann to pray for her intentions, though the ladies were present as long as he was in the room.[30]

(5) Weichmann said that after the detectives who searched the house on the night of the assassination had gone, and while the ladies were still in the parlor, he heard Miss Surratt say, "Oh ma! Just think of that man's having been here an hour before the assassination! I am afraid it will bring suspicion upon us." And he said that Mrs. Surratt

[25] *Ibid.*, I, 393.

[26] Pitman, *The Trial,* 116.

[27] *Ibid.*, 420.

[28] *Surratt Trial,* I, 715–16, testimony of Honora Fitzpatrick. Same in II, 746, testimony of Olivia Jenkins.

[29] *Ibid.*, II, 746, testimony of Olivia Jenkins.

[30] *Ibid.*, II, 747, testimony of Olivia Jenkins; *Surratt Trial,* I, 716, testimony of Honora Fitzpatrick.

Execution of the conspirators
The condemned, *left to right:*
Mrs. Surratt, Payne, Herold, Atzerodt

Photograph from the Brady-Gardner Collection
Courtesy National Park Service

replied that Booth was just an instrument in the hands of God to punish a proud and licentious people.[31]

No one else heard either the exclamation or the response.[32]

(6) Weichmann testified that at breakfast the next morning he said he had his suspicions and was going to the government to do what he could to bring suspicious parties to justice.[33]

No one else heard this remark, and when John Holahan tried to tell what was said at breakfast, he was not permitted to say more than that he did not hear any such remark as Weichmann claimed to have made.[34]

Under questioning, Weichmann admitted he might have said that as a witness at this (Surratt) trial he intended to do all he could to aid the prosecution, as his character was at stake. When Weichmann was asked if he had ever stated that he was told that unless he testified to more than he had, the government would hang him, too, the prosecution objected; the question was repeated, and Weichmann answered, "At this trial?" Asked if he had not said this in the presence of Mr. Maddox and others, Weichmann denied it.[35]

James Maddox and James J. Gifford, two Ford's Theater employees, were put on the stand to testify that they had heard Weichmann threatened. Their answers were

[31] *Ibid.*, I, 395.
[32] *Ibid.*, I, 717.
[33] *Ibid.*, I, 395.
[34] *Ibid.*, I, 674.
[35] *Ibid.*, I, 420, 449.

stricken from the record on the ground that they did not relate to the Surratt trial.[36]

By far the most damaging to Weichmann was Louis Carland's testimony. Carland, former costumer at Ford's, told how he, Weichmann, and John Brophy had taken a walk together after the conspiracy-trial testimony closed. According to Carland, Weichmann's mind was "burdened with what he had done," and he quoted Weichmann as saying, "If he had been let alone . . . it would have been quite a different affair with Mrs. Surratt than what it was."

Carland testified that Weichmann had confessed that his statement had been written out for him, and that he was threatened with prosecution as one of the conspirators if he did not swear to it. Carland said the confession was wholly voluntary on Weichmann's part.[37]

Weichmann, under examination, admitted conversing with Brophy and Carland and admitted that he had "talked the whole thing over" with Carland.[38] But he denied making the confession attributed to him. Still, he did admit that he had told these men that on one occasion Mrs. Surratt called her son aside in Weichmann's presence and said, "John, I am afraid there is something going on here. Why do these men come here? Now John, I do not feel easy about this, you must tell me what you are about." Weichmann said, "Whether John disclosed his business or not I do not know. I afterwards asked her what business John was engaged in, and she said he told her he was engaged in cotton speculations."[39] Weichmann admitted he had

[36] *Ibid.*, II, 820.
[37] *Ibid.*, II, 816–17.
[38] *Ibid.*, I, 455–57.

wanted to go to Richmond to continue his religious studies —although there was no college there.[40] Weichmann also admitted that he had talked as a secessionist with the Confederate Howell, and that he (Weichmann) was a coward.[41]

Richard Merrick, counsel for John Surratt, pointed out that no attempt was made to impeach Louis Carland or to show that Carland had any interest in the case "except his sense of justice." Merrick challenged the opposition to impeach Carland;[42] the challenge was not taken up.

Now this entire retrial of the mother at what was properly the trial of the son puts the whole matter in a peculiar legal position. It was never even established to which of the trials (the Surratt or the earlier conspiracy trial) the statements about Weichmann's being threatened referred. But the evidence presented became public property; considerable light was thrown on the characters of Weichmann and Lloyd; and there is no reason to believe that the men who testified to things embarrassing to Weichmann were actuated by anything other than a desire to tell what they themselves had heard or seen.

One other man who had been in prison with Lloyd and Weichmann was called to the stand at the Surratt trial. John T. Ford, owner of the theater where Lincoln was killed, was put on the witness stand but was permitted to say little. He did remark, of Weichmann's testimony, "I was affected by his evidence at the military court. It rather startled me that he should contradict to such an extent his

[39] *Ibid.*, I, 455.
[40] *Ibid.*, I, 455.
[41] *Ibid.*, I, 456, 459.
[42] *Ibid.*, II, 1245.

statements made to me."[43] As it stood, this remark meant little, and the prosecution should have objected to it as open to any possible interpretation.

But John T. Ford had much more to say. In a letter to the New York *Tribune* on September 2, 1873, he brought into the open for the first time the question whether Mrs. Surratt was manacled at her trial. And, in the *North American Review*, in April, 1889, Ford added further comments. He said that he was imprisoned with Lloyd and Weichmann and "was, by what I heard from them, convinced of [Mrs. Surratt's] innocence." Ford stressed that both Mrs. Surratt and the two witnesses were strangers to him at the time. He said the witnesses

> were early conspicuous in their expressions of terror to most inmates of Carroll Prison. Many yet living may recall their fright. Weichmann sought advice from the writer, saying that Secretary Stanton had, in a threatening manner, expressed the opinion that his [Weichmann's] hands had as much of the President's blood on them as Booth's.[44]
>
> The memories of my contact with these witnesses without whose testimony there was no shadow of a case against Mrs. Surratt, made the announcement of her conviction . . . a fearful horror. I deemed it a duty to devote every moment, up to the time she was doomed to die, to an effort to have her sentence commuted.[45]

Ford wrote the President asking that the sentence be

[43] *Ibid.*, II, 835–36.

[44] John T. Ford, "Behind the Curtain of a Conspiracy," *North American Review*, Vol. CXLVIII (April, 1889), 484.

[45] *Ibid.*, 485.

suspended until he could make a statement. He gave a letter to Montgomery Blair, who told him later that President Johnson saw the letter. Ford himself tried in vain to get into the White House on the day of the execution; he did not leave town until after the woman was dead.[46]

Ford closed with this justification: "I have felt it my duty to speak what I deem the truth for the memory of a lady whom I saw thrice in my life . . . and of whom I never heard until her great trouble. . . . I am striving in my humble way to do justice to her memory."[47]

It should be noted that Ford had been much incensed by being kept in the Old Capitol for nearly forty days after the assassination of Lincoln, and that he protested strongly (but in vain) when the War Department seized his theater when he tried to reopen it, July 11, 1865.[48] This fact should be kept in mind in evaluating Ford's statement, but it does not necessarily cast doubt upon his sincerity of purpose in Mrs. Surratt's behalf.

Returning to the Surratt trial, it was in the course of that trial that the plea for clemency on the behalf of Mrs.

[46] *Ibid.*, 485.

[47] *Ibid.*, 493.

[48] Ford got considerable support when he protested the seizure of his property. E. L. Godkin's *Nation* protested with him; Edward Bates thought that if Stanton could do this he might transfer estates from one man to another or dissolve marriage ties; Orville Browning thought that Ford was helpless, without means to redress himself—in a "*free* country." See *The Nation,* July 20, 1865, 65. Bates, *Diary*, entry of July 5. Browning, *Diary*, II, entry July 13. Greeley's *Tribune* expressed the hope the government would buy the building. This was done, in 1866, at a cost of $100,000.

Surratt first came to light. On August 1, Surratt's counsel twitted Edwards Pierrepont, chief counsel for the government, about the plea, as there had been rumors that such a thing existed. Two days later it was actually brought into court, only to be thrown down on a desk unexamined, and then to be retrieved by Judge Advocate General Holt and carried back to the War Department.[49] But for the first time it was clear that the rumor of such a plea was no rumor but a fact. It seemed a small thing, but important consequences followed.

The President became involved in a controversy over that clemency petition, a controversy so bitter and prolonged that Judge Holt had to strive throughout the rest of his long life to clear his name of the charge that he had suppressed the plea. In the next chapter the long and unpleasant dispute will be followed in some detail, and an attempt will be made to decide whether the President or his Judge Advocate told the truth in this matter.

[49] *Surratt Trial*, II, 1207 ff.

CHAPTER V

Mrs. Surratt—Guilty or Innocent?

Was Mrs. Surratt guilty?

BEFORE an attempt is made to answer that question, we must understand clearly the status of the two men who gave testimony against her. If pressure was brought to bear on these men—as there is reason to believe it was—it is necessary to find out how vulnerable they were. Our first concern, here, then, is with John Lloyd and Louis Weichmann.

Some government officials had no doubt about the guilt of John Lloyd. Detective Cottingham told Colonel Burnett that Lloyd was an accessory before and after the fact.[1] Lloyd had concealed arms before the murder; he had provided the fugitives with arms after the murder; and when detectives came by his tavern on the morning after Lincoln

[1] George Cottingham, statement about Lloyd, May 14, 1865, Archives, JAO, Trunk 10, "C," 245.

was shot, Lloyd denied having seen anyone[2] and sent the detectives along the Piscataway road—the road leading back to Washington.[3]

As for Weichmann, Colonel Foster thought it "extremely improbable" that Weichmann was ignorant of the plot, "if he was not an accomplice." Foster said it was "presumed" that Weichmann had spoken mysteriously before his fellow clerks in the War Department of large amounts of money to be made, in an effort to get them to join the plot.[4] Weichmann had brought John Surratt into the office after working hours.[5] According to Captain Gleason and other of his fellow-workers, Weichmann had spoken of large sums of money to be made by shady means, if he wanted to use such means, and of designs on the President entertained by a group he knew.[6] He was taught a secret Confederate cypher by the blockade-runner Howell,[7] talked as a secessionist to Howell,[8] and probably gave him information regarding the number of prisoners in Northern camps.[9] He was very intimate with John Surratt; they

---

[2] Report by Captain A. C. Richards, Metropolitan Police, to Colonel Burnett, May 9, 1865, Archives, RG 153, JAO Box No. 3, "R," 279.

[3] Detective John Clarvoe, *Surratt Trial,* I, 701.

[4] Colonel Foster's report on Weichmann, Archives, RG 153, JAO, "W" RB, 100.

[5] Statement of Gilbert Raynor, Archives, RG 153, JAO, Box No. 3, "R," RB, 75.

[6] Captain D. H. L. Gleason, Archives, RG 153, JAO, Box 1, "G" RB, 23.

[7] Testimony of Weichmann, Pitman, *The Trial,* 119; testimony of Howell, 133.

[8] Testimony of Weichmann, *Surratt Trial,* I, 456.

shared the same bed when Surratt was in town. When Payne was captured, he was wearing a pair of boots lent to Weichmann by a fellow-clerk.[10] Gleason recalled that Weichmann had mentioned Surratt and Booth in connection with vague "designs" on the President. The government had every reason to hold the opinion later expressed by Henri B. Sainte-Marie, who knew both Weichmann and Surratt and who betrayed Surratt into the hands of the United States government in 1866. Sainte-Marie felt "one was as guilty as the other" and that Weichmann "acted only through fear in selling his accomplice."[11]

With all these facts against them known to the government, Lloyd and Weichmann were understandably shaken. Lloyd's state of fear was brought out clearly at the conspiracy trial, when it was shown that, after he had been arrested and was on his way to Washington, he stopped by his home. He threw his hands around his wife's neck, cried freely, and shouted, "I am to be shot! I am to be shot!" and asked for his prayer book.[12] Weichmann's own words also show the state of his agitation. In a letter to Colonel Burnett from Carroll Prison, on May 5, 1865, he wrote:

I have the honor to call your attention to the following

[9] Testimony of Howell, Pitman, *The Trial,* 133. Colonel William Wood undoubtedly informed the government of this at the time. See Eisenschiml's quotation of Wood's later comments: *In the Shadow,* 186.

[10] Captain D. H. L. Gleason, *loc. cit.*

[11] 39 Cong., 2 sess., *House Executive Document No. 9,* dispatch from Rome, June 21, 1866.

[12] Pitman, *The Trial,* testimony of arresting officer Cottingham, 124. Also testimony of all who were present.

additional facts in my recollection. You confused and terrified me so much yesterday that I was almost unable to say anything.

I am as anxious as you and the Government are that all guilty parties should be brought to justice and meet the fate they so well deserve, but for God's sake do not *confound* the innocent with the guilty.[13]

In addition to threats, promises were used. Lloyd's admission should be conclusive in his case and has already been set forth in connection with the Surratt trial. As for Weichmann, within a month after the conspirators were hanged, he wrote Stanton asking for a job in a customhouse or post office, and, by December, he had gotten the job requested.[14] He wrote to the special commission distributing the rewards for the capture of the assassins, in the hope of monetary reward for his part in the capture. In the course of his letter he wrote, "The government has indeed been very kind to me, for through the indefatiguable exertion of Judge Holt, I was lately appointed to a position in the customs house of this city."[15]

In February, 1866, evidently having received no reply, Weichmann wrote to Judge Holt informing the Judge he had written the commission and asking Holt to look into the matter.[16] In a private letter written in 1900, Weich-

[13] Louis J. Weichmann, letter dated May 5, 1865, Archives, RG 153, JAO, Box 3, "W" RB, 102.

[14] Weichmann to Stanton, Archives, RG 153, JAO, Box 3, "W," 2065, August 16, 1865.

[15] Weichmann, Archives, JAO, Trunk 10, Item 2220 W, 1865.

[16] Weichmann, Archives, JAO, Trunk 10, Item 2220 W.

mann wrote that he had been twenty-three years in the government "at the request" of Stanton and Holt and said that without Colonel Burnett and John Bingham, "I would long ago have fallen by the wayside."[17]

Now Lloyd and Weichmann were not evil men; they were only weak men placed in an unenviable position. A chronological examination of their statements as we still have them in the Judge Advocate's Office is revealing. Lloyd did not at first implicate Mrs. Surratt. He first did so to Detective Cottingham,[18] who obtained the confession "through strategy," as he said at the conspiracy trial. What that strategy was came out at the Surratt trial.

And Weichmann, far from implicating Mrs. Surratt, at first revealed that he had heard the conversation at Uniontown between her and Lloyd—which he denied at the conspiracy trial.[19] He said that Mrs. Surratt, on her second trip to Surrattsville, went in relation to real estate. He said she left a "package of paper" at Lloyd's, and that he knew "of no other business transacted at Lloyd's only in relation

[17] Weichmann, in a letter to Dr. George L. Porter, August 15, 1900. Printed in Mary Porter, *The Surgeon in Charge*, 17.

[18] Cottingham wrote Major O'Beirne from Robeystown, as he was bringing Lloyd to Washington: "My dear Major, Mr. Lloyd has made an additional confession. He states that Mrs. Surratt called upon him in the day time Friday before the murder was committed and told him to have the firearms ready as they would be called for late that night. . . ." This is the first time this story of firearms is heard from Lloyd. Archives, JAO, Trunk 10, "C," 289.

[19] Weichmann to Colonel Wood upon being committed to Carroll Prison, statement of April 30, 1865, Archives, RG 153, JAO, Box 3.

to real estate."[20] How different the statements of these two men were later will be apparent to the reader.[21]

There are indications that both men were much troubled in conscience by what they had done. When Lloyd died in 1892, the New York *World* reported:

> Lloyd was the principal witness against Mrs. Surratt. . . .

[20] Weichmann to Colonel Wood, Archives, RG 153, JAO, Box 3, April 30, 1865.

[21] There is much interesting evidence, too lengthy to cite here, still on file in the Archives, throwing light on Weichmann's testimony. For instance, Brophy had charged that some of Weichmann's statements were written out for him. There is a statement on file marked "Items not brought out in the examination of Weichmann, which he has since recalled," which for the first time sets forth the story that Mrs. Surratt was nervous on the night of the assassination. It begins: "On the evening of the 14th Mrs. Surratt was more nervous than I ever saw her. She paced the floor of the parlor, counting her beads. . . . [*sic*] While counting her beads she asked Weichmann . . ." Here we may note the change from "I" to the third person. This is odd. And according to this same paper, Anna Surratt said "at the breakfast table next morning," "Think of that man Booths having called at this house not more than one hour and a half before the assassination." This was not heard of before and was not used at the conspiracy trial; it was used by Weichmann in his post-trial letter to Pitman in August, 1865—except that according to the letter the remark was made in the parlor on the night of April 14. See Pitman, *The Trial,* 421. As we have seen, at the Surratt trial, no one else in the room heard the remark. Yet the source of these two stories about Mrs. Surratt is a single-page paper, apart from a prepared statement by Weichmann, marked "Items not brought out in the examination of Weichmann or that he has since recalled," and giving some evidence of having been written out for him to sign.

Although Lloyd's testimony was most damaging against Mrs. Surratt, and probably condemned her, he himself never believed in Mrs. Surratt's guilt, and said she was a victim of circumstances. Her associations with the real conspirators, he always held, was the cause of her conviction.[22]

There are two versions of Weichmann's death. One is that before he died he signed a statement declaring that all he had said at the conspiracy trial was true;[23] the other version is that Weichmann, for some obscure reason, died unshriven.[24]

But the testimony of Lloyd and Weichmann apart, it remains to be seen if Mrs. Surratt was innocent. To answer this question it is necessary to answer two separate questions: Did Mrs. Surratt know of the abduction plot? Did she know of the plot to kill the President?

Did she know of the abduction plot? Post-trial statements by those connected with the case are not much help in answering this question. John Clampitt believed she knew

[22] New York *World*, December 22, 1892.

[23] Lloyd Lewis, *Myths After Lincoln*, 267. Lewis quotes what he was told by Weichmann's sisters; this was never substantiated by the signed statement.

[24] Mrs. Helen Jones Campbell, in a letter to the writer, June 12, 1951. Mrs. Campbell's source is an affidavit given her by a priest who knew Weichmann's elder brother, Father Weichmann, who heard the confession but did not give absolution, according to this source.

This whole story makes little sense. Weichmann had studied for the priesthood; his brother was a priest; yet a third priest is said to have been asked to grant absolution—an impossible request. As Monsignor McAdams says, "It goes against the grain." McAdams, conversation with the writer, August 2, 1951.

nothing of any such plot.[25] Frederick Aiken, on the other hand, believed she did.[26] Benn Pitman agreed with Aiken in this.[27] Another court reporter, E. V. Murphy, agreed with Clampitt on her innocence.[28] Clearly, it is not in comparing opinions that an answer may be found.

The evidence is this: Payne exonerated Mrs. Surratt of any part in the abduction plot.[29] Samuel Arnold did likewise.[30] Weichmann, who certainly knew a great deal about the plot (if he did not know all), did not know that Mrs. Surratt ever knew of it. Neither John Holahan (against whom nothing suspicious was ever found) nor Anna Surratt ever heard mention of any plot against the President.[31]

At the conspiracy trial Weichmann told how he came home from the office one day during Payne's second visit at Mrs. Surratt's and found Mrs. Surratt weeping bitterly.

[25] Clampitt, *loc. cit.*, 226.

[26] G. A. Townsend, "The Widow Surratt," Aiken to Townsend, unidentified newspaper clipping.

[27] Pitman, "Benn Pitman on the Trial of Lincoln's Assassins," *Tyler's Quarterly Historical and Genealogical Magazine*, Vol. XXII, No. 1 (July, 1940), 11, 15.

[28] Edward V. Murphy, *New York Times Magazine* (April 9, 1916), 8.

[29] Payne's statement is suspect, in that he felt responsible for Mrs. Surratt's trouble because he was found at her house when she was arrested. But his sincerity convinced all who heard him, and his story that John Surratt warned the plotters against speaking in his mother's presence gains some support from Weichmann's admission that he did not know that she knew what was afoot in her house.

[30] Arnold, *loc. cit.*

[31] Pitman, *The Trial*, 131, statement of Anna Surratt; 139, John Holahan's statement.

He said she told him, "John is gone away." He went on to tell how, about six o'clock, Booth, John Surratt, and Payne came in very much upset and then dispersed. Weichmann quoted the Negro servant as saying seven men had ridden out from Mrs. Surratt's that day.[32] This story refers, of course, to the abortive abduction attempt. It is Weichmann's unsupported statement, but no effort was made to refute it, so it is difficult to tell how much credence it deserves. Clara Laughlin probably gave the most reasonable interpretation of this story in her book, *The Death of Lincoln,* when she speculated that, if the story is true, John had probably left his mother a note telling her of the plot. Miss Laughlin felt that "to the unprejudiced mind" it looked as though, had Mrs. Surratt known of the plot all along, she would have learned to control her emotions before mid-March and, if she approved of the design, would have rejoiced.[33]

Of the plotters, Atzerodt and Payne had stayed at the boardinghouse. Atzerodt stayed one night only, and Weichmann afterward heard Anna Surratt say she didn't care about having "such sticks" brought to the house, as they were not proper company for her—and Mrs. Surratt agreed.[34] Payne came to the house in March and stayed

[32] *Ibid.,* 118, Weichmann's testimony. It seems improbable that seven men rode out from Mrs. Surratt's that day, whether or not Mrs. Surratt was weeping when Weichmann got home from the office. If Samuel Arnold is to be believed, he and O'Laughlin rode out from their livery stable, and Arnold, at least, had no idea Mrs. Surratt lived in Washington, until the trial. Arnold, *loc. cit.*

[33] Laughlin, *op. cit.,* 47–48.

[34] Pitman, *The Trial,* 116, Weichmann's testimony.

one night, returning three weeks later to stay three days.[35] When Payne came to the house he posed as a Baptist preacher and gave his name as "Wood." Weichmann heard Mrs. Surratt say he was a "great looking" Baptist preacher.[36] When Payne first came to the house, we have Weichmann's word that Mrs. Surratt did not recognize him. Weichmann took Payne up to his own room and took supper up to him[37] —though the man had given his name as "Wood" to Mrs. Surratt, he told Weichmann his name was Payne.[38] All of which suggests far more against Weichmann than it tells us about Mrs. Surratt.

In short, there is no proof that Mrs. Surratt knew what was being plotted in her boardinghouse. According to her daughter, Mrs. Surratt said, when told that a stranger (Payne) was at the door, that she did not understand why strange persons should call there, but she supposed their object was to see her son, and she would treat them politely.[39] There is no stronger evidence against her than this: that she suspected something but could not imagine why strange men kept calling on her son. Her involvement in the abduction plot cannot be more than a guess.

Did Mrs. Surratt know of the plot to assassinate Lincoln? Again, post-trial statements show some variation. Two of her judges—Generals Harris and Wallace—never believed her innocent.[40] Aiken and Clampitt agreed that she

[35] *Ibid.*, 114, 116.
[36] *Ibid.*, 115.
[37] *Surratt Trial*, I, 376, Weichmann's testimony.
[38] Pitman, *The Trial, 114*, Weichmann's testimony.
[39] *Ibid.*, 131, testimony of Anna Surratt.
[40] Harris, *Assassination of Lincoln*, chapter entitled "The

Prison yard, Old Penitentiary.
Photograph taken after the execution

Photograph from the Brady-Gardner Collection
Courtesy National Park Service

was innocent, here.[41] Two of the court reporters were in agreement, also. Pitman wrote, "That she was wholly innocent of the crime for which she was hanged I have never changed my belief since I compiled the last page of my book."[42] Murphy wrote that every action of the woman's life and her exemplary character cried out against her complicity and "against the 'deep damnation of her taking off' on the purchased and perjured testimony of two interested and discredited witnesses."[43]

One act of Mrs. Surratt was most damaging to her. On the day of the assassination she had delivered a package from Booth to Lloyd. There is nothing to imply that this was more than a favor innocently granted. Weichmann reported her "lively and cheerful" on the drive to Surrattsville that day. There is nothing to show that she was expecting or received a caller that night—indeed, she set out for church after dinner but was turned back by threatening weather.[44] Her conduct was not unusual in the parlor that night—according to everyone but Weichmann. Her behavior that day and night strongly suggests complete ignorance of Booth's scheme.

As Booth told Payne, Herold, and Atzerodt of his plot to kill Lincoln only two hours before the deed, it would

Case of Mrs. Surratt." Lewis Wallace, *Lew Wallace: An Autobiography*, II, 848.

[41] Townsend, "The Widow Surratt," Aiken to Townsend; Clampitt, *loc. cit.*, 226.

[42] Pitman, "Benn Pitman on the Trial of Lincoln's Assassins," *Tyler's Quarterly Historical and Genealogical Magazine*, Vol. XXII, No. 1 (July, 1940), 12.

[43] Murphy, *loc. cit.*

[44] *Surratt Trial*, I, 689, testimony of Eliza Holahan.

be surprising if he had told Mrs. Surratt six hours earlier. And since he never saw her again after he asked her to take the package to Lloyd, it is difficult to imagine what he would have gained by entrusting his secret to her. That she was innocent of any part in the assassination is as certain as anything can be which is not subject to absolute proof.[45]

Mrs. Surratt's own words are still to be heard. Two of her statements have been preserved. Of Booth, she said she did not know how her son came to meet him, but that she was not surprised that he should make his acquaintance "because I consider him capable of forming acquaintances in the best society."[46] She said she had no idea what brought her son and Booth together, and she added, "I think no one could be more surprised than we were that he should be guilty of such an act. We often remarked that Mr. Booth

[45] Colonel William Wood took the witness stand to testify in Mrs. Surratt's behalf; and, according to his friend, Thomas Nelson Conrad, Colonel Baker "confessed in writing that he had destroyed certain records, which contained evidence to prove Mrs. Surratt's innocence, and that document is still extant and in possession of the man to whom it was given, Colonel William P. Wood." According to Conrad, Wood had the necessary evidence to show that Weichmann had given information to the Confederacy, but this was among the papers Baker destroyed. Conrad asserted that Wood had been monitoring mail going South from Mrs. Surratt's, up to just before the assassination, and that there was no hint of assassination in it. See Thomas N. Conrad, *Confederate Spy*, 125, 133, 130. Such secondhand evidence is difficult to evaluate. Where it can be checked against Wood's published statements, it is in harmony.

[46] It should not be forgotten that Booth moved in the "best society" before the assassination. He knew members of Congress and was affianced to a senator's daughter.

was very clear of politics; he never mentioned anything of the kind, and it was a subject that was never indulged in." Asked her political sentiments, she replied, "I don't pretend to express my feelings at all; I have often said that I thought the South acted too hastily; that is about the amount of my feelings, and I say so again."[47]

Asked about Payne, Mrs. Surratt's version of their meeting the night they were arrested is of interest. She said:

He was a tremendous, hard fellow with a skull-cap on, and my daughter commenced crying and said these gentlemen came to save our lives. I hope you arrested him.

Q. Did you have any arrangement made with such a person as to do anything about your premises?

A. I assure you I did not.

[47] Whatever Mrs. Surratt's political sentiments, she was very discreet about expressing them. No one came forward at the conspiracy trial to testify to her disloyalty; many came forward to testify to her loyalty. She had fed Union soldiers and received no money for it; yet she had one son who had gone South and one who was running the blockade. Her political feelings were probably pro-Southern, and she may have known of John Surratt's blockade-running; but neither of these things can be conclusively proved. John was away a great deal in the winter of 1864–65, "down in the country," it was generally said at the conspiracy trial. Mrs. Surratt said she encouraged him to be away, because she thought he was better off in Maryland than in Washington, where there were restaurants and "bad company." But when she was making this statement, she had every reason to cover up for her son; she had no reason to admit he had ever been to Richmond, or that she knew of his having gone. We may suppose that she knew; Brophy said Weichmann heard her weep and implore him not to go. This secondary evidence is the best available; it can hardly be considered definitive.

Q. He tells me now that he met you in the street and you engaged him to come to your house.

A. Oh! Oh! It is not so, Sir; for I believe he would have murdered us every one, I assure you.

Q. Did he have anything in his hand?

A. He had some kind of a weapon.

Q. When did you see him first?

A. Just as the carriage drew up; he rang the door bell, and my daughter said: "Oh! there is a murderer."[48]

Of her conversation with Lloyd on the afternoon of the assassination, Mrs. Surratt said she was in her buggy when he drove up, and that she did not get down. According to her, Weichmann heard the conversation between Lloyd and herself. Asked if she knew any guns were hidden at the tavern, she replied, "No Sir, I did not."[49] Asked, "Did your son or Mr. Booth or Herold or Port Tobacco [Atzerodt] ever tell you that they had engaged in a plot to kill the President?" Mrs. Surratt replied, "Never in the world if it was the last word I have ever to utter."

Mrs. Surratt declared her innocence in a brief, scrawling note to a friend on the day of her execution. Requesting the friend to stay with her daughter that day, she said, "God knows I am innocent but for some cause I must suffer today."[50]

[48] Mary E. Surratt, statement of April 17, 1865.

[49] Mary E. Surratt, statement of April 28, 1865. John Clampitt's belief was that Mrs. Surratt delivered a package for Booth which contained arms, and that he told her what the package contained, though, in Clampitt's opinion, the act was an innocent favor on Mrs. Surratt's part. Clampitt, *loc. cit.*, 227–28.

[50] Mary E. Surratt, photostatic copy of the letter, Library of

If Mrs. Surratt was not guilty (and there was and is a reasonable doubt), why was she hanged?

In the immediate background of her execution is the question of the suppression of the clemency petition in her behalf. What was the petition and the argument over it? In brief, it was as follows:

The official record in the Archives gives no clue to the circumstances which produced this plea.[51] The members of the commission trying the conspirators met June 29, 1865, to consider the findings. It is evident that five of the nine martial judges had reservations about hanging Mrs. Surratt. John Clampitt later asserted, "It was at first proposed (and I have it on the most credible authority) to acquit Mrs. Surratt, or at least to spare her life." But, he says, the Judge Advocate objected.[52] Assistant Advocate Bingham drew up the petition "at the request of a member of the court," according to General Harris.[53] On July 5 Judge Holt took a special "Brief Summary" of the trial testimony and (he claimed) the plea into the White House, where he saw President Johnson alone. The President approved the findings, and Mrs. Surratt was hanged.

When the clemency petition was brought out at the trial

Congress, Manuscript Division, Personal Papers, Misc. Cf. Lafayette C. Baker's report of a confession allegedly made to him by Mrs. Surratt admitting her complicity in the abduction plot and her reluctant yielding to Booth's urgings to aid him in the assassination. It should be noted Baker first made public this "confession" in his book in 1867, and it is generally regarded as spurious. Baker, *History of the United States Secret Service*, 563.

[51] It gives the findings; the plea follows, without comment.

[52] Clampitt, *loc. cit.*, 239.

[53] Harris, *Assassination of Lincoln*, 114.

of John Surratt, President Johnson sent to the War Department for it. On August 5, 1867, Johnson's private secretary, Colonel W. G. Moore, noted:

The president, having heard that there was a recommendation in favor of Mrs. Surratt, sent today for the papers. . . . Forwarded with the papers was a recommendation of the court for a commutation of the sentence in the case of Mrs. Surratt from hanging to imprisonment for life. The President emphatically declared that he had never seen the recommendation. He was positive to me the circumstances attending the signing of the order. . . . He distinctly remembered the great reluctance with which he approved the death warrant of a woman of Mrs. Surratt's age, and that he asked Judge Advocate General Holt, who originally brought the papers to him, many questions, but nothing whatever was said to him respecting the recommendation for clemency in her case. . . . Besides, the recommendation did not appear in the published proceedings of the trial, by Benn Pitman, prepared and issued by authority of the Secretary of War and he felt satisfied it had been designedly with-held from his (the President's) knowledge.[54]

The petition, subject of so much recrimination, read:

The undersigned, members of the Military Commission detailed to try Mary E. Surratt and others for the Conspiracy and the murder of Abraham Lincoln, late President of the United States, respectfully pray the President, in consideration of the sex and age of the said Mary E. Surratt, if he can, upon all the facts in the case, find it consistent with his sense

[54] Colonel W. G. Moore, "Notes," *American Historical Review*, Vol. XIX (October, 1913), 108.

of duty to the country, to commute the sentence of death, which the Court have been constrained to pronounce, to imprisonment in the penitentiary for life.

Respectfully submitted

(Signed) D. Hunter, August V. Kautz, R. S. Foster, James A. Ekin, Chas. H. Tompkins.[55]

For half a dozen years after the clemency plea came to public view, nothing more was heard of it. Then Judge Holt published his "Vindication" in the Washington *Daily Morning Chronicle* on August 25, 1873, giving letters from various persons to substantiate his claim that he showed the plea to President Johnson. John Bingham wrote that Stanton had told him that the plea had been before the Cabinet and the President, and that the Cabinet "were a unit" in denying it. Bingham said he asked Stanton if he could make this revelation public but was told not to do so. (Stanton was dead and, as Holt pointed out, had never publicly said anything.) Former Attorney General Speed wrote that he would not speak of proceedings before a Cabinet meeting, but he would say that he saw the record in the President's office and that the petition for clemency was attached. Former Secretary of the Interior James Harlan wrote that he thought there was an accidental meeting of several members of the Cabinet—perhaps only three or four of them. Harlan distinctly recalled only Stanton and Seward. One of these, he said, was addressing the President, saying, "Surely not, Mr. President, for if the death penalty should be commuted in so grave a case as the assassination of the head of a great nation on account of the sex

[55] Original in the Archives, *Restricted Material.*

of the criminal, it would amount to an invitation to assassins hereafter to employ women as their chief instruments." Rev. J. G. Butler, St. Paul's Church, Washington, D. C., wrote that he had talked with Johnson a few hours after the execution, when Johnson made his much quoted remark about Mrs. Surratt having kept the nest that hatched the egg. Johnson also told him (said Butler) that no plea was made for Mrs. Surratt except her sex, and that to have interceded on that ground would have been to have licensed female crime. These were the highlights of the "Vindication."

On November 12, 1873, President Johnson answered Holt.[56] He asked why Holt did not get from either Stanton or Seward "evidence so essential to his reputation" before their deaths in 1869 and 1872, respectively. He pointed out that Harlan admitted that no part of the record was ever read in his presence. Johnson also declared that, in passing on the sentence of Mrs. Surratt, the fact that she was a woman suggested mercy. If it did so to five members of the military commission, "is it strange that in the absence of any petition whatever, it also suggested itself to the Executive?" Johnson asked. He pointed out that the petition could not have been considered in a Cabinet meeting, as he had been ill and no meeting was held until Friday. Yet, Bingham had said that the clemency plea was considered by the Cabinet before it gave its approval of the death sentence. Johnson said Speed must be mistaken, because he and Judge Holt examined the papers alone, and Holt took them away with him—so Speed could not have seen the

[56] Andrew Johnson, in the Washington *Daily Morning Chronicle*, November 12, 1873.

papers or the petition in Johnson's office, as he claimed. Johnson says Holt "urged with peculiar force and solemnity" that to favor Mrs. Surratt would be to encourage females to engage in crime, and that he (Holt) thought the time had come to set an example. Then Johnson came to his most convincing argument: the fact that no mention of the clemency plea was made in Pitman's official record:

although in addition to the proceedings of the court . . . the book contains an appendix, giving, among other matters . . . affidavits made on the 11th of August, 1865, more than a month after the execution and diagrams of the locality of Ford's theater, and of its stage. . . .If, as Judge Holt asserts, it was a crime to suppress or conceal it from the President, was it not also a crime designedly to omit this important page from his authorized version of the trial? It cannot be claimed the omission was accidental, for, according to Judge Holt's witnesses, the paper, as soon as signed, was attached to the record.

Johnson thus ends on this note: Holt can take his choice; either he gave a false record to the public, or he suppressed it from the President.

Having said that when he saw the papers in August, 1867, he was convinced that the plea was missing from the record when Holt brought it to his office in 1865, Johnson left no doubt as to where he stood on the issue.

Judge Holt soon after made a "Rejoinder" to Johnson. Holt said he delayed in speaking out because he was collecting testimony, and because he didn't know any member of the Cabinet knew of the matter, this having been kept from him by Stanton. He contended that the informal meeting

Harlan mentioned must have taken place July 5 or 6.[57] He said he had urged nothing on Johnson, but that Johnson fixed the early date of the execution to avoid "opportunity for criticism, remonstrances, . . ." He said Pitman omitted the plea because "recommendations to mercy . . . do not in law constitute any part of the records." Pitman, in a letter to Holt, said the plea was not inserted because it formed no part of the trial.[58]

Holt ended by saying he thought the public would believe him, "and, if truth has power to disarm the cloud of calumny . . . I may feel that for the future this cloud can have no terrors for me."

But Holt spent the rest of his life trying to clear his name. In 1888—thirteen years after his resignation as judge advocate general—he made public his correspondence with James Speed on this subject.[59] In a series of letters to Speed in 1883, Holt begged him to speak out, and so clear his

[57] Former Secretary of the Navy Welles wrote Johnson on November 5, 1873, remarking that it was clear from his diary that there was no Cabinet meeting until July 7, and further, that he himself had never seen the plea or heard it discussed at any time. See Andrew Johnson Papers, Library of Congress, Manuscript Division, Vol. 159, Item No. 25819. Holt never appealed to Welles on this issue, though Johnson did not use this letter by Welles or even mention Welles.

[58] In 1912 Pitman admitted that he never saw this plea, "but I have good reason to believe it was made"—an interesting, if belated, admission. Pitman, "Benn Pitman on the Trial of Lincoln's Assassins," *Tyler's Quarterly Historical and Genealogical Magazine, Vol.* XXII, No. 1 (July, 1940), 19.

[59] Judge Holt, "New Facts about Mrs. Surratt," *North American Review,* Vol. CXLVII (July, 1888), 83–94.

(Holt's) name. Holt, in his first letter, pleaded piteously his advancing years and asked Speed to remove the cloud hanging over him.

Speed begged off for six months on various excuses and, finally, in late August, said he could not say more than he had already said. Holt, two months later, wrote reminding Speed that in 1873 he had claimed to have seen the plea in the President's office; Holt added that he had "learned" that "at the moment I laid before the President the record of the trial, with the recommendation on behalf of Mrs. Surratt, you chanced to be so situated as to be assured by the evidence of your own senses that such petition . . . was by me then presented to the President."

Speed, on December 26, wrote that he was sorry, but that when Johnson was still alive he had offered to Holt to speak—if Johnson gave his consent. Holt, in a footnote, flatly said that nothing of this sort ever happened.

From all this, it appears that if Speed knew anything, he was spying on Holt and Johnson when they believed themselves alone in Johnson's office. As Johnson pointed out, that was the only time the plea was in his office. But Speed had claimed, in 1873, that he had seen the plea there. Thus Speed either did not wish to admit spying, or the original claim was untrue. The difficulty of making either admission probably explained Speed's strange reticence in the face of the aged Judge Holt's anguished efforts to get him to speak out.

This still leaves unanswered the question whether Johnson saw the plea. Probably the answer to that lies in the physical appearance of the plea itself. When Judge Holt drew up the order of execution to be signed by Johnson, he began writing under the signature of David Hunter at the end of the record. The page was filled before he had finished, but instead of turning the page up and continuing to write on the back from the bottom down (the usual method followed on the other pages), he turned the entire record over and went on writing on the back page from its top down. DeWitt long ago pointed out that this change, intentional or not, would put any leaf flying loose at the end of the record (as the clemency petition probably was) out of sight of the President when he signed the record.[60] After examining the papers, a related question suggests itself to the writer. If Holt did take the petition into the President, and if he did not hide it, why doesn't the writing of the so-called death warrant begin after the last name on the clemency plea, instead of where it does begin, after the last name on the last page of the report of proceedings? This presumes that the plea would be found at the end of the report—the most reasonable place for it to be found. Of course, if Holt had not taken the plea into the President, it is clear why he began writing where he did. But the strange way Holt turned the sheets over leads one to believe DeWitt was right. In either event, Holt seems to be condemned by the physical appearance of the petition.

This is not to say that President Johnson would have commuted the sentence if he had known of the petition. Johnson never hinted that he would have acted otherwise had he known of the petition, and in 1873 he still classified Mrs. Surratt as one of the assassins. He quite properly relied on his Judge Advocate General and his Secretary of

[60] DeWitt, *Assassination of Lincoln*, 137.

War, and these two did not serve him faithfully in this instance.

Why was Mrs. Surratt hanged? Why did Stanton and Holt suppress the petition for clemency in her behalf? These questions are far more difficult than the questions relating to the degree of Mrs. Surratt's guilt, and, it may be, they will never be answered completely and satisfactorily. But some clues may be found in the characters of the men and in the temper of their times.

Gideon Welles had observed Judge Holt's "strange weaknesses." He thought Holt credulous "and often the dupe of his own imaginings." He noted that Holt held "men guilty on shadowy suspicions, and is ready to condemn them without trial." Welles noted that "Stanton has sometimes brought forward singular papers relating to conspiracies, and Holt has assured him in his suspicions."[61] In regard to a wartime organization known as The Sons of Liberty, Judge Holt was a special alarmist; a later historian remarked that Holt was "credulous to the extent of accepting as truth nearly all the statements of detectives and alarmists."[62] Temperamentally these two men were not ideally suited to ride out the storm of emotion and confusion that followed the assassination.

Stanton and Holt became convinced of Southern complicity in Lincoln's assassination. Stanton was warned by General Dix that Sanford Conover, whose testimony had helped establish the government's case against the Confederacy, had been a special agent of the rebel government in Canada, under the name of Wallace; that he was the

[61] Welles, *Diary*, II, 424.

[62] Rhodes, *op. cit.*, V, 327.

Montreal correspondent of the New York *Times,* the *World,* and the *News* under three different names; that he had been imprisoned at Richmond under the name of Charles A. Denham, which was probably his real name; that his character "in other respects" was bad; and that his testimony would have no weight "unless corroborated by witnesses of unquestionable credibility."[63] Eight prominent citizens of Windsor, the home of James Merritt, another witness against the Confederacy, swore Merritt was a fraud, and the *Toronto Globe* of June 24, 1865, gave sworn statements of three justices of the peace branding Merritt a quack.[64] Yet the Secretary of War and his Judge Advocate General ignored these warnings and accepted at face value all statements by Conover and Conover's witnesses. In so doing, they caused the new President to brand, "without the slightest warrant," seven Southern leaders, who were "as innocent of the murder as himself, of complicity in the foulest crime of the age," as the English magazine *Blackwood's* observed at the end of Johnson's term in office.[65]

Also, Holt and Stanton are frequently alleged to have been prejudiced against Southern women and Catholics. This allegation is much more difficult to prove than it is to assert. John Brophy alleged that Weichmann told him that Stanton's hatred of Catholics and Southern women "would be Mrs. Surratt's undoing," and that "he could no nothing

[63] General J. A. Dix, letter to Stanton from New York, June 24, 1865. Stanton Papers, Vol. 27, Library of Congress, Manuscript Division.

[64] 39 Cong., 1 sess., *House Report No. 104,* 39.

[65] "The Outgoing and the Incoming President," *Blackwood's Magazine,* Vol. CV (April, 1869), 451.

to help her." Brophy also said Colonel LaFayette Baker told him Stanton and Holt were both "ready to convict any Catholic on whom suspicion might fall."[66] General Mussey wrote that President Johnson remarked that clemency to Mrs. Surratt was urged solely upon the grounds of her sex, and that he (Johnson) thought there hadn't been "women enough hanged in this war."[67] If Johnson said this (and he never denied it), it is unlikely that he meant Northern women, and Mrs. Surratt could have hoped for little succor for a Southern woman, even if the President had seen the plea for clemency and even if Holt and Stanton had had no animosity toward Southern ladies.

Several of the defendants were Catholic, and it would not be surprising if anti-Catholic prejudice entered into the minds of the martial jurists at the conspiracy trial. However, only one of these jurists ever openly declared that he was suspicious of Catholic involvement in the assassination.[68]

In looking back over the case now, the biggest factor in Mrs. Surratt's death seems to have been political. In fact, there were two trials going on in May and June of 1865—the trial of the prisoners in the dock, and the trial of the Southern leaders for conspiracy. The two stories unfolded daily in the newspapers, side by side. Developments in one paralleled developments in the other. This is strikingly evi-

[66] John P. Brophy, *Washington Post,* Jan. 7, 1908.

[67] General Mussey to Holt, letter dated Aug. 19, 1873. In Holt's "Vindication" of August 25, 1873, in the Washington *Daily Morning Chronicle.*

[68] In 1897 General Harris wrote a book to establish his thesis. He called it *Rome's Responsibility for the Assassination of Lincoln.*

dent from a study of contemporary newspapers. Throughout the trial, the rebel conspiracy overshadowed everything else. The papers were full of headlines about the complicity of Jefferson Davis, "Jake" Thompson, and others. The papers broadcast the testimony given at the trial about military attempts made on New York during the late war; about conditions in Libby and Andersonville prisons; the St. Albans raid; the attempt to burn New York, and so on. There was no scarcity of this kind of news.

It must be remembered that the Southern leaders were named in the charge against the prisoners in the dock at the conspiracy trial. Special Judge Advocate John Bingham missed no opportunity to "rake the whole Confederacy, from Jeff Davis all down the line to the prisoners at the bar," as a friendly observer[69] recalled many years later, and as the records of the trial make abundantly clear. Nothing was too irrelevant to be brought into the record and to be carried in the newspapers later, after it had been heard in the courtroom. A lawyer, writing in *Green Bag*, a magazine for lawyers, reviewing the case, remarked, "No lawyer of experience in criminal jurisprudence can now read the testimony . . . without arriving at the conclusion that, if it had been offered in calm times before a learned court, the great bulk of it would have been excluded either on the ground of incompetency or irrelevance—and mainly on the latter ground." And he went on to observe, "The Military Commission seemed to be not only ascertaining the guilt . . . but also educating public sentiment of the North as to the

[69] Watts, *loc. cit.*, 95. Watts defended the military commission and its constitutionality, although in later years he had become a judge in Adrian, Michigan. Date of Watts' comment: 1914.

tional Union

ERNOON, JULY 7, 1865.

TRA.

matter on every page.

n!—The Constitutional
I!—Ourselves!!!
ession of names to the
l of The Constitutional
prevent that immediate
rompt delivery of the pa-
ere we desire. We are
anising the routes in or-
e certainty of the receipt
by all who may wish to
o them daily.
ave reached us recently
many of our subscribers
aper regularly. This dif-
st to be able to entirely
earnestly desiring to se-
al delivery of the paper,
nation to leave no effort
asure that very important
the purpose, then we may
thoroughly perfect our
bviate all difficulty and
n annoying complaint in

ish The Constitutional
daily will oblige us by
ames to the Publication
be remembered the price
ered daily, is *only* Ten
t.
friends who have Adver-
ny kind and for any pur-
r us with their patronage.
daily increasing circula-
Constitutional Union
luable medium to reach
ody. Business men may
ts columns to secure good
ers.

Freedmen.—Col. Brown,
of Freedmen for Virginia,
ess to the colored people
on the Fourth of July,
em with regard to their
ells them that, having
ed placed in a position to
oceeds of their labor, it
em to answer to the world
will be industrious and
take care of themselves.
them the protection and
the Government, and all
n their efforts, and warns
idleness and vagrancy,
h no leniency will be
ds are to be established
of the benefits of which
lished to avail themselves,
eminded of the great re-
hich now rests upon them
destiny of their race.

from John C. Breckin-
C. Breckinridge writes a
ba to Hon. E. M. Bruce, a
late Confederate Congress,
1865, from which the fol-
racted: "I have heard no
outer world since I dis-
Woodstock, Ga., the last
ce east of Chattahoochie.
ill be wisdom enough in
t Washington city not to
nd suffering people to the
pring from despair. Every
w exert all the influence
make the present cessa-
be permanent and honora-
be remembered that there
ing peace founded upon
pression."

Admiral Dupont.—Ad-
, U. S. N., whose unex-
is so deeply mourned by
nt and the country, be-
s will the sum of one hun-
nty-five thousand dollars
for the education and relief
children of the sailors and
republic, soon to be organ-
gton by an act of Congress.
ount of Admiral Dupont's
ring his brilliant services
tlantic blockading squad-
possessed of a handsome
wn.

Bureau.—Gen. Howard
report from two agents of
it out to travel through
e, purpose of informing
and employe as to their
es, and to give them such

2nd Edition.

THE EXECUTION AT THE ARSENAL.

Mrs. Surratt, Payne, Herold, and Atzerodt Hung—Unsuccessful Attempt to Stay the Execution.

APPROACHING THE ARSENAL.

Pickets and guards were stationed up Four-and-a-half street the whole length of the Island, and approaching the arsenal the number of the guard increased. About twenty yards in front of the outer gate a cordon of troops was stationed across the passage way, with an officer to examine all who desired to enter the precincts of the prison. At the first gate was stationed Lieutenant Townsend, of Company A, 9th V. R. C.

Upon entering the outer gate the wide expanse of space was covered with hundreds of field pieces, and on the left, looking south, was observed a battalion of troops under arms, and on the right rested the 8th regiment First Army Corps, commanded by Colonel Pierce. Detachments of the 1st, 2d, and 3d regiments of First Corps were also on the ground. The river bank was crowded with troops enjoying the fresh breeze blowing from the river. Staff officers and orderlies were dashing around on horseback, as though important events were at hand.

A great quiet prevailed, and it seemed as though the very elements partook of the awful scene soon to take place. The guard and detached soldiers spoke in whispers—in fact, a death-like calm was the predominating feature.

The old Penitentiary building loomed up across the extended space, sombre and gloomy, with sentries pacing the high walls, and sentries in the walk below. On the west side were some twenty A tents, with troops lounging around. At the south gate, the principal entrance, and formerly the old carriage way, was another guard drawn up, with a captain in command, who again scrutinised the passes.

Upon entering the prison-yard, the 1st regiment 1st corps, Colonel Charles Bird, were under arms, and doing guard duty around the gallows. Major Stegran and Surgeon Sheldon were also on duty there. This is the regiment just returned from the Wilderness, where they have been engaged in burying the dead of those fearful battles that took place in that vicinity.

Soldiers were around the prison pump filling their canteens, and officers were lunching in the shade—they not having broken their fast until 11 o'clock, at which time the carpenters were finishing off the gallows, and laborers carrying off the extra lumber.

THE GALLOWS.

This is entirely a new structure, built very strong, with heavy timbers. The gallows proper, consisted of three heavy upright beams, with a cross-piece, to which dangled four ropes, one much longer than the other—evidently to be used in hanging Payne. The traps or platforms were two in number, and very ponderous, and made for two prisoners each. These traps were supported by two upright posts, which upon a given signal, were to be knocked down by a battering ram, thus launching the condemned into eternity. The gallows was reached by a wide pair of steps or double steps, with a rail extending up them and around the whole gallows, with the exception of that portion where the traps were.

The four ropes dangled in the breeze, with the regular hangman's knots balancing them.

Inside the prison the deepest silence prevailed. At one of the windows on the east side of the main prison, the curious were looking in, where the condemned cells were directly opposite. The first cell, No. 151, contained Atzerodt, No. 153 Mrs. Surratt, No. 155 Herold, and No. 157 Payne. In front of these cells were a guard. Their spiritual advisers were with the prisoners, and the low hum of their devotion was perceptible to the ear from without.

Very few people were in the corridor, outside the guard and their officers.

East of the gallows were four pine boxes to be used as coffins, piled up one upon the other, and north of these were four rough graves dug, side by side, close to the wall. They were four feet deep and about three feet wide.

TESTING THE GALLOWS.

About half-past 11 o'clock workmen commenced to test the platforms or traps, with huge weights. The left hand trap, facing south as the traps are built, did not work or fall clearly, stopping at about two feet fall. This was soon remedied, and the traps dropped clear. The sound of these experiments, a roar or grating sound accompanying each, must have been heard by the prisoners.

At this time, half-past 11 o'clock, the civilians began to arrive in numbers. The sun shone very hot, and there was but little shade in the prison yard.

At 12 o'clock the guard was placed on the walls, in one rank, close order, preparations evidently being made for the execution. The carpenters at this time altered the arrangements for knocking the props from beneath the traps, by shortening the props or stanchions, and placing a raised base beneath, so they could act with more surety.

Miss Surratt and a gentleman took leave of Mrs. Surratt just previous to her execution. She appeared to be perfectly resigned to her fate. Her daughter was with her all night. The daughter was overburthened with sorrow, and her exclamations of grief were quite heart-rending.

At ten minutes to one o'clock the chairs for the condemned to rest upon while on the scaffold, were carried out of the prison. General Hancock, deeply impressed, was overlooking all the arrangements through a grated window opposite the west side of the gallows.

THE EXECUTION.

At one o'clock preparations commenced for the execution, Gen. Hancock, with an aid and Mrs. Surratt's counsel Messrs. Aiken & Clampitt, came out a side door, and in a moment after came Mrs. Surratt, led or supported by Col. McCall and a sergeant. Mrs. Surratt wore a black bonnet, with a heavy black veil. She also wore a long black dress, which dragged on the ground. Her arms were bound behind, as well as her ancles.

Atzerodt followed Mrs. Surratt, with his two spiritual advisers, Rev. F. G. Butler and Rev. W. W. Winchester. He was dressed in a shabby suit of grey mixed goods, without hat, and on his feet he wore blue cloth slippers.

Herold followed with the Rev. M. L. Olds, of Christ Church. Payne came last, standing erect and firm, and looked like a sailor man, being costumed in a blue suit and straw hat. Payne was attended by Rev. Dr. A. D. Gillette, of the First Baptist Church, and the Rev. A. P. Stryhen.

Previous to leaving her cell, Mrs. Surratt declared her innocence, and stated that God in Heaven knew she was innocent. It was said by many present that Payne made a confession last night, and exonerated her, Mrs. S., of all complicity in the conspiracy.

Soon the condemned were all seated on the gallows, Father Walter and Father Wiget administering consolation to Mrs. Surratt, who fervently kissed the cross.

Mrs. Surratt and Payne were on the same trap, and Atzerodt and Herold on the other.

After the reading of the order of execution by General Hartranft, the Rev. Dr. Gillette stated that Lewis Powell or Payne sincerely thanked all whom he has had dealings with since his arrest, as he had been treated with great kindness. A prayer followed these remarks by the doctor. Payne at the close bowed and muttered "amen."

M. L. Olds followed with a supplication for Herold, and then the Rev. J. G. Butler for Atzerodt—the prisoner all the while moving his lips in prayer.

Atzerodt was the first to receive the rope around his neck, Herold next, then Payne, and after some delay in tying the dress of Mrs. Surratt, she received the rope.

After this, strings of white muslin were used in tying or making more secure the arms and legs of the condemned. Payne held his neck up high to receive the noose, and was the first to receive the white cap, Atzerodt next, Herold next, and Mrs. Surratt last. While securing the others, Atzerodt, with his face covered cried out, "gentlemen take war—," and just before the trap fell, again cried out, "good bye gentlemen; may we all meet in another world."

Payne acted more like a quiet spectator than a man for execution; Mrs. Surratt was very nervous, and requested, just before the final scene, her supporters not to let her fall; Atzerodt looked pale and shakey, and Herold wore quite a troubled countenance.

Very little was said after the prayers, and at twenty-five minutes past 1 o'clock, two soldiers knocked the props from beneath the traps, when they fell with a *thud*. Mrs. Surratt died without a struggle—in fact, it is more than likely she was not at all conscious when she was launched into eternity. Atzerodt also died very easy; but Herold struggled violently for a moment or so, and Payne not quite so hard. The bodies swayed to and fro for some time, and the left hand of Mrs. Surratt seemed as though it were clutching at the right, and now and then Herold's legs would be drawn up—likewise Payne's.

Shortly after the execution the military cleared the grounds of all civilians.

The bodies will be delivered to the friends of the executed; and if not called for will be interred in the graves already dug.

Outside the prison cake and lemonade venders were around as though they were attending a holiday.

The only female we saw present was Miss Major Walker, Sugeon. When she left the Penitentiary, she rode her horse as a man does.

Payne spent the night well, Atzerodt was very nervous, and Herold slept for several hours. His mother and sisters attended him. Mrs. Surratt was sick all night, and quite prostrated up to the time of the execution.

No civilians were allowed in the prison building, and every shady nook in the yard was occupied with a guard, and the spectators suffered intensely from the sun.

AN ATTEMPT TO STAY THE EXECUTION!

At an early hour this morning Mr. Aiken, one of the counsel for Mary E. Surratt, applied to Judge Wylie, of the Supreme Court of this District, for a writ of *habeas corpus* to stay her execution to-day.

It was granted, and directed to Major General Hancock to produce her in court at 10 a. m. to-day.

Shortly after 10 a. m. the Marshal made return that General H. had resured to obey the writ, &c.

At noon Gen. Hancock, accompanied by attorney General Speed, appeared in court, and the case was taken up, the return read, &c. It embraced General Hancock's reply in writing, stating that the President had suspended the power of the writ in this case, as he had done in several previous cases, by virtue of the law of Congress authorising him so to do; and directing him to make no obedience to the order of the court, for which reason he declined to do so.

His reply was accompanied by various military orders in the case, embracing the President's action in the premises.

The Court, in a few remarks, explained that the military authorities having taken the case out of its hands, it had no power to proceed further in it.

Attorney General Speed addressed the Court briefly in explanation of the action of the government in the premises, showing that the suspension of the writ of *habeas corpus* was absolutely necessary in time of war for the preservation of the public liberties and the life of the Government in time of peace, and [illegible] the right of the military authority to protect the life of the commander-in-chief of the army and navy and through its own courts in such times.

He declared that the Government had given the case anxious consideration, and had directed that the writ should not be complied with only after mature and patriotic deliberation. He also expressed his confidence that Judge Wylie had been guided in the matter only by sincere convictions of duty.

The Court responded to his remarks, in further explanation of the necessity resting upon it to take no further action, &c.

Financial and Commercial.

Gold closed last evening at Gallahers New York Stock Exchange at 139¼.

The New York *Times*, of yesterday, says:

"The Stock Exchange after the Fourth of July vacation opened with some signs of firmness, and a good business was done in the Railways and also in the Miscellaneous Shares at the early Board. At a later hour, on Broad-street, (Open Board of Brokers,) the full prices of the morning were not quite sustained, though the general tone of the market continued steady. At the Second Board, the Railway biddings were irregular—lower on New York Central, Erie and Reading, and firm for Michigan Southern and Illinois Central. The Government Stocks opened at 104⅛@104¼ for the 5-20s, and gained strength through the dealings of the day, clearing 105 ℔ cent, for the old issue, and 104¼ for the new. Other descriptions of United States Gold-bearing Stocks were steady. The European demand continues to run almost exclusively on the original 5-20s, and although the whole issue amounts to $514,780,500, the

The *Constitutional Union's* account of the execution.
Extra, second edition, Friday, July 7, 1865

alleged conspiracy of confederate officials with the assassination."[70] He felt that the effect of Bingham's oratory was "in one aspect an appeal to the excited galleries of the American people provided by stenographers and newspapers."[71]

Whether or not this interpretation is correct, sectional feelings ran high at the trial. When one considers the evidence before the court—that there was but one plot against the President's life, that Mrs. Surratt had twice asked John Lloyd about "shooting irons," and that her son was hardly less guilty of the crime than John Wilkes Booth himself—it is not surprising that Mrs. Surratt was hanged. What is surprising (and to the credit of these Union officers who sat upon her trial) is that a majority of the court signed a plea for clemency in her behalf.

If Judge Holt suppressed the clemency plea which a majority of these officers had signed (as there is reason for believing he did), one can only guess at his motives. He was probably influenced by his strong, well-known Unionist sentiments (whether or not he hated Southern women), by the firm belief (whether or not mistaken) that the woman was guilty, and by frustration at not being able to lay hands upon her son. This last factor may have been most important, for both Stanton and Holt must have found it galling that one whom they believed so guilty should have eluded them.

Probably the most telling factor in Holt's mind was that he believed her guilty. He was throughout his public

[70] A. O. Hall, "The Surratt *Cause Célèbre*," *Green Bag*, Vol. VIII (May, 1896), 197.

[71] *Ibid.*, 198.

life a rather stern, rigorous man.[72] The Washington *Evening Star* reported, when Holt died, that he could not stand to see animals suffer—he would not permit hunting on his place in Kentucky—but that he was "rigid" in his belief "that reasoning beings should be held to a strict accountability for their actions."[73]

Holt's superior, Stanton, must, of course, share the responsibility for the death of a woman whose guilt was never more than a guess. But Stanton never publicly commented on the Surratt case, and speculation about his motives is rather futile. If he had any secrets—or explanations—he took them to the grave with him after his death on Christmas Eve, 1869.[74]

[72] He recommended hanging Milligan, Bowles, and Horsey without reservation, though Lincoln did not act upon his recommendation. Rhodes, *op. cit.*, V, 328.

[73] Washington *Evening Star*, August 1, 1894.

[74] Colonel Wood, who visited him on the day before his death, reported Stanton's remorse over having hanged Mrs. Surratt. There is no corroborative information. See Eisenschiml, *In the Shadow*, 187.

Bibliography

[An asterisk precedes the items of especial value]

Primary Sources

Manuscripts and Archival Material

*Booth, J. W. *Diary*. This diary is now on display in the Lincoln Museum (old Ford Theater) in Washington.

**Capture and Trial of the Lincoln Conspirators*. Five volumes of clippings, Washingtoniana Division, Washington Public Library.

*Library of Congress: Manuscript Division.

Corcoran, W. W. Papers. Especially Vol. 12.

Hardie, General J. A. Papers. One manuscript box.

Holt, Judge Joseph. Papers. Especially Vol. 69.

Johnson, Andrew. Papers. Vols. 61–70, 153.

Johnson, Reverdy. Papers. One red manuscript box.

Stanton, Edwin M. Papers. Especially Vols. 26–27.

Surratt, Mary E. Papers. One item (photostatic copy).

National Archives.

**Court Martial of the Lincoln Conspirators*. Records of the Judge Advocate General, War Department Records Section, MM 2251. This is the official transcript of the trial, about five thousand pages in longhand, written from the shorthand stenographic reports taken in the courtroom. It is restricted material.

District of Columbia Archives. Records of the District Court, Habeas Corpus No. 46.

**Record Group 153*. Records of the Judge Advocate General, War Department Records Section, Records Relating to the Lincoln Assassination Suspects, April, 1865. This item consists of boxes numbered one, two, and three. It includes statements made by the accused, by witnesses for the prosecution, and by various persons concerned with the capture of Booth or with the conspiracy trial.

**Trunk Ten*. Office of the Judge Advocate General, War Department Records Section. *Trunk Ten* contains material relating to the distribution of rewards offered for the capture of J. W. Booth.

Raymond, Colonel Julian E. "History of Fort Lesley J. McNair."

Register of Prisoners, Old Capitol, Military Department of the District of Columbia. This is a multivolume record giving names and data on prisoners placed in the Old Capitol Prison.

Government Documents and Publications

39 Cong., 1 sess., *House Report No. 104*. Majority and minority reports of the Judiciary Committee investigating the assassination of Abraham Lincoln (July, 1866).

39 Cong., 2 sess., *House Exec. Doc. 9*. This item relates to reports and correspondence leading to the capture of John H. Surratt.

**Congressional Globe*. See especially the Thirty-ninth and Fortieth Sessions of Congress.

Impeachment Investigation. 40 Cong., 1 sess., *House Report No. 7.* Government Printing Office, 1868. Set forth here is the transcript of testimony of witnesses at the Andrew Johnson impeachment trial investigation.

The War of the Rebellion, Official Records of the Union and Confederate Armies. 70 vols. Washington, Government Printing Office, 1899–1901. See especially Series I, Vol. XLVI, Part 3, and Series II, Vol. VIII.

United States Code, 1946 edition, Title 28, Sec. 632 (Act of March 16, 1878, 20 Stat. 30).

Secondary Sources

Newspapers

*New York:

Evening Post
Herald
Times
Tribune
World

The files of these papers were examined for April–July, 1865.

*Richmond *Whig,* April, May, 1865.

*Washington:

Constitutional Union, April–July, 1865.
Daily Morning Chronicle, April–July, 1865; September 19, 1873; August, November, December, 1873.
Evening Star, April–August, 1865; November–December, 1873; April 14, 1894; August 1, 1894.
Herald, April–July, 1865.
National Intelligencer, April–July, 1865.
Post, July 21, 1901; January 7, 1908.

Articles

Arnold, Samuel A. "The Lincoln Plot," *Baltimore American* (1902). In Lincoln Clippings, Washingtoniana Division, Washington Public Library.

Barbee, David R. "They Couldn't Escape American Justice," *Washington Post Magazine* (May 6, 1934).

———. "Why Mrs. Surratt Was Not Spared," Washington *Evening Star*, February 12, 1949.

Burnett, H. L. "Controversy Between President Johnson and Judge Holt." Paper read at a meeting of the Commandery, State of New York Loyal Legion (April 3, 1889). Printed in full in T. M. Harris, *Assassination of Lincoln, q. v.*

*Clampitt, John W. "Trial of Mrs. Surratt," *North American Review*, Vol. CXXXI (September, 1880), 223–40.

Croffut, W. A. "Lincoln's Washington," *Atlantic Monthly*, Vol. CXLV (January, 1930), 55–65.

Doherty, E. P. "Narrative," *Century Magazine*, Vol. XXXIX (January, 1890), 443–49.

Ford, J. T. "Behind the Curtain of a Conspiracy," *North American Review*, Vol. CXLVIII (April, 1889), 484–93.

———. Letter to the New York *Tribune*, Sept. 2, 1873, signed "Truth."

Forney, D. C. "Thirty Years After," Washington *Evening Star*, June 27, 1891.

Gleason, D. H. L. "Conspiracy Against Lincoln," *Magazine of History*, Vol. XIII (February, 1911), 59–65.

Gray, John A. (ed.). "Fate of the Lincoln Conspirators," *McClure's Magazine*, Vol. LXXXII (October, 1911), 626–36.

Hall, A. O. "The Surratt *Cause Célèbre*," *Green Bag*, Vol. VIII (May, 1896), 195–201.

Holt, Joseph. "New Facts about Mrs. Surratt," *North American Review,* Vol. CXLVII (July, 1888), 83–94.

*———. "Refutation," Washington *Daily Morning Chronicle,* December 1, 1873. Reprinted as pamphlet under the title *Rejoinder.*

*———. "Vindication," Washington *Daily Morning Chronicle,* September 3, 1866. Reprinted as pamphlet.

*Johnson, Andrew. Letter to the editor answering Holt's "Vindication," Washington *Daily Morning Chronicle,* November 12, 1873.

King, Horatio. Letter to "Topics of the Time," *Century Magazine,* Vol. XXXIX (April, 1890), 955–57.

McDevitt, James A. "Some Interesting Reminiscences of a Thrilling Night," *Evening Star,* April 14, 1894.

Mason, V. L. "Four Lincoln Conspiracies," *Century Magazine,* Vol. LI (April, 1896), 889–911.

*Moore, Colonel W. G. "Notes," American Historical Review, Vol. XIX (October, 1913), 98–132.

Murphy, Edward V. *New York Times Magazine* (April 9, 1916), 8–9.

*"The Out-going and the Incoming President," *Blackwood's Magazine,* Vol. CV (April, 1869), 449–65.

"Payne the Assassin," *Harper's Weekly,* Vol. IX (May 27, 1865), 321.

Pitman, Benn. "Benn Pitman on the Trial of Lincoln's Assassins," *Tyler's Quarterly Historical and Genealogical Magazine,* Vol. XXII (July, 1940), 1–22.

Proctor, J. C. "Lincoln's Days of Tragedy," Washington *Sunday Star,* April 11, 1937.

Southern Historical Society. "The Treatment of Prisoners During the War Between the States." Compiled by the secretary of the Southern Historical Society, *Southern Historical Society Papers,* I (1876), 112–326.

Speed, John. *North American Review*, Vol. CXLVII (September, 1888), 314–19.

Stone, Frederick. New York *Tribune*, April 17, 1883. Interview.

Townsend, G. A. "The Widow Surratt." Aiken interview. Unidentified newspaper clipping.

*Walter, Rev. Jacob A. Remarks made before the United States Catholic Historical Society. *Church News*, A Catholic Family Journal, Washington, August 18, 1891. Clipping in Toner Collection, Library of Congress.

Watts, R. A. "The Trial and Execution of the Lincoln Conspirators," *Michigan History Magazine*, Vol. V (1922), 81–110.

Wilson, H. "E. M. Stanton," *Atlantic Monthly*, Vol. XXV (February, 1870), 234–46.

Periodicals

**Blackwood's Magazine*, April–July, 1865.

**Harper's New Monthly Magazine*, April–July, 1865.

**Harper's Weekly*, April–July, 1865.

**Leslie's Illustrated Weekly*, April–July, 1865.

**The Nation*, July, 1865.

Books

*Amator Justitiae. *Trial of Mrs. Surratt: or contrasts of the past and present*. (Pamphlet.) Dated June 14, 1865, Washington. An impassioned plea for Mrs. Surratt. Author uncertain.

Andrews, Marietta M. *My Studio Window*. Sketches of the Pageant of Washington Life. New York, E. P. Dutton and Company, 1928.

**Assassination of Abraham Lincoln*. Expressions of Condolence and Sympathy Inspired by These Events. Washington, Government Printing Office, 1866. Expressions of Condolence received by the State Department following Lincoln's assassination.

Assassination and History of the Conspiracy. Cincinnati, J. R. Hawley and Company, 1865.

Baker, Lafayette C. *History of the United States Secret Service*. Philadelphia, L. C. Baker, 1867.

Bates, David H. *Lincoln in the Telegraph Office*. New York, Century Company, 1907.

*Bates, Edward. *Diary*. *Annual Report* of the American Historical Society, IV, 1930.

Battles and Leaders of the Civil War. New York, Century Company, 1884–87.

Bingham, John A. *Trial of the Conspirators*. Washington, Government Printing Office, 1865.

*Browning, Orville. *Diary*. Ed. by T. C. Pease and J. G. Randall. Lincoln Series, Vols. II–III, Illinois State Historical Library, 1925–33.

Bryan, George S. *The Great American Myth*. New York, Carrick and Evans, Inc., 1940.

Buckingham, J. E. *Reminiscences and Souvenirs of the Assassination of Abraham Lincoln*. Washington, Rufus H. Darby, 1894.

Butler, B. F. *Butler's Book*. Boston, A. M. Thayer and Company, 1892.

Campbell, Helen Jones. *The Case for Mrs. Surratt*. New York, G. P. Putnam's Sons, 1943.

Chesnut, Mary Boykin. *A Diary from Dixie*. New York, Peter Smith, 1929.

Chittenden, L. E. *Recollections of President Lincoln*. New York, Harper and Brothers, 1891.

Clay, Mrs. C. C. *A Belle of the Fifties*. New York, Doubleday, Page and Company, 1904.

Coggeshall, E. W. *Assassination of Lincoln.* Chicago, W. M. Hill, 1920.

Conrad, Thomas N. *Confederate Spy.* New York, J. S. Ogilvie, 1892.

Crook, W. H. *Memories of the White House.* Boston, Little, Brown and Company, 1911.

———. *Through Five Administrations.* New York and London, Harper and Brothers, 1907.

Dana, Charles A. *Recollections of the Civil War.* New York, D. Appleton and Company, 1898.

Davis, Jefferson. *Rise and Fall of the Confederate Government.* 2 vols. New York, D. Appleton and Company, 1881.

Davis, Varina H. *Jefferson Davis.* A Memoir. New York, Belford Company, 1890.

*DeWitt, David M. *The Assassination of Abraham Lincoln and Its Expiation.* New York, The Macmillan Company, 1909.

———. *The Judicial Murder of Mary E. Surratt.* Baltimore. J. Murphy and Company, 1895.

Dodd, W. E. *Jefferson Davis.* Philadelphia, G. W. Jacobs and Company, 1907.

*Doster, W. E. *Lincoln and Episodes of the Civil War.* New York and London, G. P. Putnam's Sons, 1915.

Douglas, Henry Kyd. *I Rode with Stonewall.* Chapel Hill, University of North Carolina Press, 1940.

Eisenschiml, Otto. *The Drama of Lincoln's Assassination.* Harrogate, Tennessee, 1937.

———. *In the Shadow of Lincoln's Death.* New York, Wilfred Funk, Inc., 1940.

———. *Reviewers Reviewed.* Ann Arbor, Wm. L. Clements Library, 1940.

———. *Why Was Lincoln Murdered?* Boston, Little, Brown and Company, 1937.

Farjeon, Eleanor (ed.). *The Unlocked Door.* A Memoir of John Wilkes Booth by His Sister Asia Booth Clarke. New York, G. P. Putnam's Sons, 1938.

Ferguson, W. J. *I Saw Booth Shoot Lincoln.* Boston and New York, Houghton Mifflin Company, 1930.

Flower, F. A. *Edwin McMasters Stanton.* New York, W. W. Wilson, the Saalfield Publishing Company, 1905.

Forrester, Izola. *This One Mad Act.* Boston, Hale, Cushman and Flint, 1937.

Grant, U. S. *Personal Memoirs.* 2 vols. New York, Century Company, 1903.

The Great Conspiracy. A Book of Absorbing Interest! Startling Developments. Eminent Persons Implicated. Full Secret of the Assassination Plot. Philadelphia, Barclay and Company, 1866.

Harris, T. M. *Assassination of Lincoln.* Boston, American Citizen Company, 1892.

———. *Rome's Responsibility for the Assassination of Lincoln.* Pittsburg, Williams Publishing Company, 1897.

Harrison, Mrs. Burton. *Recollections Grave and Gay.* New York, Charles Scribner's Sons, 1911.

Hertz, Emanuel (ed.). *The Hidden Lincoln.* From the letters and papers of W. H. Herndon. New York, Blue Ribbon Books, Inc., 1940.

*Holt, Joseph. *Rejoinder*. Washington, 1873. This pamphlet is a reprint of a letter from Holt to Andrew Jackson.

*———. *Vindication* of Judge Advocate General Holt from the foul slanders of traitors, confessed perjurers and suborners, acting in the interests of Jefferson Davis. Washington, 1866.

*———. *Vindication* of the Honorable Joseph Holt, Judge

Advocate of the United States Army. Washington, Washington Chronicle Publishing Company 1873. Note that there were two different *Vindication* pamphlets. The first defended Holt's name in his conduct of the trial of the conspirators; the second set forth letters from various persons to prove that Holt did not suppress the clemency plea on behalf of Mrs. Surratt.

Howard, Hamilton. *Civil War Echoes.* Washington, Howard Company, 1907.

Julian, G. W. *Political Recollections.* Chicago, Jansen, McClurg and Company, 1884.

Kimball, Judge I. G. *Recollections.* Washington, Carnahan Press, 1912.

Kimmel, Stanley. *The Mad Booths of Maryland.* New York, Bobbs-Merrill Company, 1940.

Lamon, Ward H. *Recollections of Abraham Lincoln.* Washington, Dorothy Lamon Teillard, 1911.

Laughlin, Clara E. *The Death of Lincoln.* New York, Doubleday, Page and Company, 1909.

Lawson, John (ed.). *American State Trials,* VIII. St. Louis, Law Book Company, 1917.

Lewis, Lloyd. *Myths After Lincoln.* New York, Harcourt, Brace and Company, 1929.

*Lomax, Virginia. *The Old Capitol and Its Inmates.* New York, E. J. Hale and Sons, 1867.

McAdams, Monsignor E. P. *History of Saint Charles Borromeo Parish,* 1849–1949. (Pamphlet.)

McCarthy, Burke. *Suppressed Truth about the Assassination of Abraham Lincoln.* Burke McCarthy, 1922.

McClure, Stanley W. *The Lincoln Museum and the House Where Lincoln Died.* (Pamphlet.) National Park Service Historical Handbook Series No. 3. Washington.

Mudd, Nettie. *Life of Dr. Samuel A. Mudd.* New York, Neal Publishing Company, 1906.

National Cyclopedia of American Biography, IV. New York, James T. White and Company, 1897.

Ogden, Rollo (ed.). *Life and Letters of Edwin L. Godkin.* New York, The Macmillan Company, 1907.

Oldroyd, Osborn H. *Assassination of Abraham Lincoln.* Washington, 1901.

*Pitman, Benn. *The Assassination of President Lincoln and the Trial of the Conspirators.* Cincinnati and New York, Moore, Wilstach and Baldwin, 1865. Pitman's abridgment of the conspiracy trial testimony. It is far from complete, but no abridgment could be entirely satisfactory.

*Poore, Ben ["Perley"]. *Conspiracy Trial for the Murder of the President.* 3 vols. Boston, J. E. Tilton and Company, 1865–66. Poore sets down the complete testimony of the conspiracy trial until June 13, 1865, when his record ends. This record is the same, word for word, as the stenographic record in the War Department Archives.

———. *Perley's Reminiscences of 60 Years in the National Metropolis.* 2 vols. Philadelphia, Hubbard Brothers, 1886.

Porter, Mary W. *The Surgeon in Charge.* Concord, New Hampshire, Rumford Press, 1949.

Riddle, A. G. *Recollections of War Times.* New York, G. P. Putnam's Sons, 1895.

Russell, C. W. (ed.). *Memoirs of Colonel John S. Mosby.* Boston, Little, Brown and Company, 1917.

Sherman, W. T. *Memoirs.* 2 vols. New York, D. Appleton and Company, 1913.

———. *The Sherman Letters.* New York, Charles Scribner's Sons, 1894.

Shotwell, W. G. *Driftwood.* New York, Longmans, Green and Company, 1927.

Stern, Philip Van Doren. *The Man Who Killed Lincoln.* New York, Literary Guild of America, Inc., 1939.

Stevens, Dr. L. L. *Lives, Crimes and Confessions of the Assassins.* Troy, New York, Daily Times Stream Printing Establishment, 1865.

Stewart, W. M. *Reminiscences.* New York, Neale Publishing Company, 1908.

Surratt, John H. *Diary.* New York, Fred Brady, 1866. (Diary believed spurious.)

Townsend, G. A. *Katy of Catoctin.* New York, D. Appleton and Company, 1886.

*———. *Life, Crime and Capture of John Wilkes Booth,* New York, Dick and Fitzgerald, 1865.

**Trial of John H. Surratt in the Criminal Court for the District of Columbia.* 2 vols. Washington, Government Printing Office, 1867.

Wallace, Lew. *Lew Wallace.* An Autobiography. 2 vols. New York, Harper and Brothers, 1906.

*Welles, Gideon. *Diary.* 3 vols. Boston and New York, Houghton Mifflin Company, 1911.

Wilson, Francis. *John Wilkes Booth.* Boston, Houghton Mifflin Company, 1911.

Wise, John S. *The End of an Era.* Boston and New York, Houghton Mifflin Company, 1899.

General Works

Beale, Howard K. *The Critical Year.* New York, Harcourt, Brace and Company, 1930.

Blaine, J. G. *Twenty Years of Congress,* 2 vols. Norwich, Connecticut, Hill Publishing Company, 1884.

Bowers, Claude G. *The Tragic Era*. Boston, Houghton Mifflin Company, 1929.

Bryan, W. B. *A History of the National Capital*. 2 vols. New York, Macmillan Company, 1914.

Dunning, W. A. *Reconstruction*. New York, Harper and Brothers, 1907.

Leech, Margaret. *Reveille in Washington*. New York and London, Harper and Brothers, 1941.

McClellan, G. B. *McClellan's Own Story*. New York, Charles Webster and Company, 1887.

McCulloch, Hugh. *Men and Measures of Half a Century*. New York, Charles Scribner's Sons, 1900.

McMaster, John B. *A History of the People of the United States*. New York, D. Appleton and Company, 1927.

Milton, G. F. *Age of Hate*. New York, Coward-McCann, Inc., 1930.

———. *Conflict:* the American Civil War. New York, Coward-McCann, 1941.

Nicolay, J. G., and John Hay. *Abraham Lincoln,* A History. 10 vols. New York, Century Company, 1890.

Oberholtzer, E. P. *A History of the United States Since the Civil War,* I. 5 vols. New York, The Macmillan Company, 1917.

Randall, J. G. *Civil War and Reconstruction*. New York, D. C. Heath and Company, 1937.

Rhodes, J. F. *History of the United States,* V. 7 vols. (1902–1904). New York, Macmillan Company, 1906.

Roberts, Chalmers M. *Washington, Past and Present*. Washington, Public Affairs Press, 1949–50.

Thayer, J. B. *Cases on Evidence*. 2nd ed. Cambridge, 1900.

Two Centuries Growth of American Law, 1701–1901. New York, Charles Scribner's Sons, 1902.

Warren, Charles. *A History of the American Bar*. Cambridge University Press, 1912.

———. *The Supreme Court in United States History*. 3 vols. Boston, Little, Brown and Company, 1922.

Wigmore, J. H. *Wigmore on Evidence*. 10 vols. Boston, Little, Brown and Company, 1940. Especially Vol. I, Sec. d, and Vol. II, Sec. 579.

Winthrop, Colonel W. W. *Military Law*. 2 vols. Washington, J. J. Chapman, 1893.

———. *Military Law and Precedents*. 1920 edition. Washington, Government Printing Office.

Index

UNIVERSITY OF OKLAHOMA PRESS

NORMAN

CPSIA information can be obtained at www.ICGtesting.com
Printed in the USA
BVOW07s1243211114

375992BV00001B/8/P